# bigCat diary Lion

# Jonathan and Angela Scott

HarperCollins*Publishers*

To Carole Wyman, whose generous spirit has touched our lives
and many others, helping to make our dreams come true.

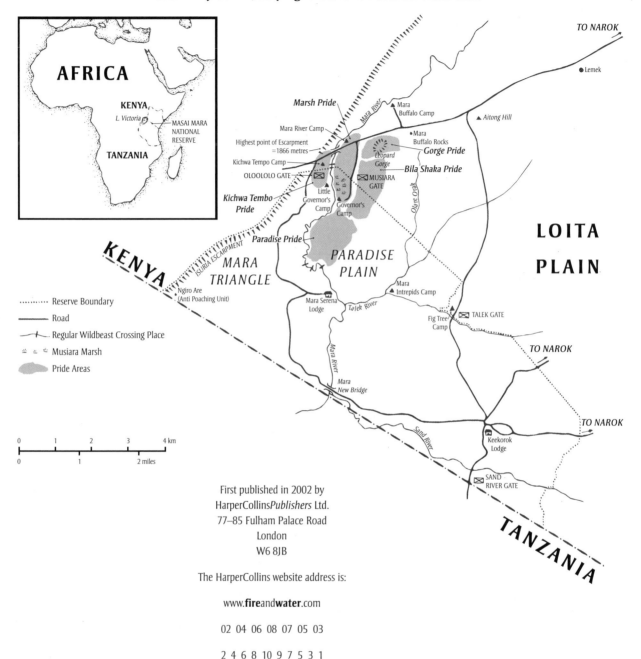

**AFRICA**

KENYA

L. Victoria

MASAI MARA
NATIONAL
RESERVE

**TANZANIA**

TO NAROK

Lemek

*Marsh Pride*

Mara
Buffalo Camp

Aitong Hill

Mara River Camp

Mara River

Highest point of Escarpment
=1866 metres

Mara
Buffalo Rocks

*Gorge Pride*

Kichwa Tempo Camp

Leopard
Gorge

*Bila Shaka Pride*

OLOOLOLO GATE

MUSIARA
GATE

*Kichwa Tembo
Pride*

Little
Governor's
Camp

Governor's
Camp

Olare Orok

**LOITA**

*Paradise Pride*

**PLAIN**

*Paradise Pride*

**MARA
TRIANGLE**

**PARADISE
PLAIN**

Ngiro Are
(Anti Poaching Unit)

Mara
Intrepids Camp

Mara Serena
Lodge

Talek River

Fig Tree
Camp

TALEK GATE

**KENYA**

ISURIA ESCARPMENT

......... Reserve Boundary

———— Road

⊥ Regular Wildbeast Crossing Place

Musiara Marsh

Pride Areas

*TO NAROK*

Mara River

Mara
New Bridge

Sand River

*TO NAROK*

Keekorok
Lodge

SAND
RIVER GATE

**TANZANIA**

| 0 | 1 | 2 | 3 | 4 km |

| 0 | 1 | 2 miles |

First published in 2002 by
HarperCollins*Publishers* Ltd.
77–85 Fulham Palace Road
London
W6 8JB

The HarperCollins website address is:

www.**fire**and**water**.com

02 04 06 08 07 05 03

2 4 6 8 10 9 7 5 3 1

ISBN 0 00 714666 3

The copyright in the photographs belongs to Jonathan and Angela Scott apart from the following: p.16 Chris Butler/Science
Photo Library, p.18 John Sibbick/The Natural History Museum, London, p.19 The Natural History Museum, London, p.22
David Scott
Maps by Caroline Simpson, reproduced with kind permission of Kyle Caithie Ltd.

Colour reproduction by Colourscan, Singapore
Printed and bound in Great Britain by The Bath Press

# Contents

# Introduction

*The large predators have now reached the twilight of their existence. Shot for so-called sport, in demand by the fur industry, trapped and poisoned because they kill both wild and domestic animals in which man has a vested interest, the tiger, cheetah, wolf and others will probably not survive except in large reserves. In the future only national parks may remain as samples of wilderness where man can renew his ancient ties with the predators that were once his competitors and with the prey that provided him with sustenance.*

George Schaller
**Serengeti: A Kingdom of Predators**

Jonathan, soundman Andy Milk and cameraman Mark Yates join members of the Ridge Pride early one morning as they feast on a buffalo kill.

Every two years during the first week in September a crew of 30 wildlife film-makers, sound recordists, presenters, driver-guides and game-spotters gather in the Masai Mara National Game Reserve in Kenya to film a new series of *Big Cat Diary*. Our base for the next ten weeks is to be a tented camp overlooking the sinuously beautiful Mara River, the perfect spot from which to strike out and follow the daily lives of the lions, leopards and cheetahs who are the real stars of the television series. By the time we reach the dining tent at five o'clock each morning the camp staff will already have been up for an hour, preparing dozens of picnic boxes: breakfast and lunch are eaten in the bush. We generally don't get back to camp until well after dark – just enough time for a hot shower ahead of dinner, and a chat round the campfire before falling into bed, taking care not to bump into one of the 2-tonne hippos which will have emerged from the river to feed around our tents. Three months from now we'll be dead on our feet, but by then they'll have to drag us out of the Mara. Nobody wants to leave. It's that kind of place.

But right now it's a piping hot cup of tea or coffee we're looking for to ward off the chill morning air. The first sounds of a dawn chorus are already ringing in our ears, the liquid song of the white-browed robin chat urging us on our way. For the rest of the day home will be the inside of a four-wheel-drive vehicle. It may be the perfect mobile hide for filming wildlife, but it's a pressure cooker of a place in the heat of the day and a magnet for hard-biting tsetse flies. That's a price worth paying if we can find Shadow the leopard or film the Marsh Lions making a kill. But there's no guarantee that anything will happen with the big cats. And many times it doesn't. That's why we keep coming back to the Mara. When the lions and leopards are sleeping there will always be something for us to film: herds of wildebeest and zebras crossing the river, elephants feeding among the acacia thickets, a troop of banded mongooses foraging for insects or the hectic social activity around a hyena den. There's nowhere quite like the Mara.

Each of the big cats we are following has its own cameraman, sound recordist and producer. The programmes are edited in a tent in the bush and at the end of each week a master tape makes its way via Nairobi to the BBC Natural History Unit in Bristol. Nothing is changed apart from adding music and titles. It's as close to real life as you can get: the ultimate big-cat soap opera.

Big cats have always inspired awe and fear among humans, none more so than the lion. As Evelyn Ames wrote in *A Glimpse of Eden*:

*Lions are not animals alone: they are symbols and totems and legend; they have impressed themselves so deeply on the human mind, if not its blood, it is as though the psyche were emblazoned with their crest. When you look into the eyes of a free lion and watch the grace of his long stride – all that extra, unused energy flowing under the skin; when you see the noble-looking calm of the mouth and nose, the proud authority of the bearded chin – the mysterious reminder of the faces of classic and mythological heroes – you recognize to your marrow that you were born with that image already in you.*

Khali's ten-week-old cubs greeting Scar, who responds by baring his huge canines to let them know he wants to be left alone.

I had to wait 25 years before I was able to see a 'free lion'. Until then my fascination with Africa's big cats had to be satisfied by annual visits to London Zoo to watch the lions at feeding time or to Bertram Mills's Circus to see them parading around the big top. Exciting as those encounters were, they simply fired my longing to travel to Africa to see big cats in the wild. When the film *Born Free* appeared in cinemas in the 1960s I remember sitting spellbound as the story of George and Joy Adamson's relationship with the lioness Elsa in the wilds of Kenya unfolded on the big screen. Here were the sights and sounds of Africa vividly brought to life: the spectacle of all those animals, the dust and the heat. Little did I realize then that I too would one day live among wild lions in Kenya.

In 1974 I set off overland from London to South Africa, armed with a degree in zoology and a thirst for a more exciting life. My first glimpse of wild Africa far exceeded anything I had dreamed of. Nothing prepares you for the moment when that first herd of elephants emerges from the riverine forests or stilt-legged giraffes glide effortlessly across the plains. But it was the thought of seeing Africa's big cats that gave

substance to my journey. Who could fail to feel inspired at the sight of a full-grown male lion standing regally at the edge of the Masai Mara's rolling grassy plains, gazing out over his kingdom, thick dark mane tussled by the wind? His yellow eyes glint in the morning light as he listens for the sound of other lions or searches the blue of the sky for signs of vultures plummeting to the ground, pinpointing the place where his pride has killed. It is a timeless scene, creating a deep sense of longing. A reminder of times past, when man competed side by side with Africa's great predators for food.

Having spent most of the past 25 years based in the Masai Mara, photographing and writing about Africa's big cats, I relished the opportunity of co-presenting the first series of *Big Cat Diary* with wildlife film-maker Simon King in 1996. I had met Simon some years earlier when he asked me to help him with background information on the Mara. He wanted to make a film on lions and had read my first book *The Marsh Lions* (co-authored with Brian Jackman), which described the life of an African pride in words and pictures. The success of that book relied on an intimate

The Marsh Lions resting in the sparse shade of a boscia tree. Lions spend 18–20 hours a day resting.

knowledge of the lions in the northern Mara and featured one pride – the Marsh Lions – that I had followed on a daily basis. Simon had made a name for himself with a series of animal dramas featuring British wildlife, as well as filming a number of wildlife specials focusing on individual animals. His lion film documented the struggles of a lioness named Khali as she attempted to raise her cubs on the fringes of the Marsh Lions' territory. *Big Cat Diary* promised Simon the chance to reacquaint himself with some of the lions he had come to know during that period.

At its best *Big Cat Diary* captures the excitement and immediacy that everyone feels on safari in Africa. In many ways it mirrors what my wife Angie (who is also a wildlife photographer) and I spend the majority of our life doing. Whenever we can, we head off on safari to the Musiara area of the northern Mara where *Big Cat Diary* is filmed, driving out each day in search of the big cats we have come to know so well. Although our knowledge of them is constantly updated by reports from

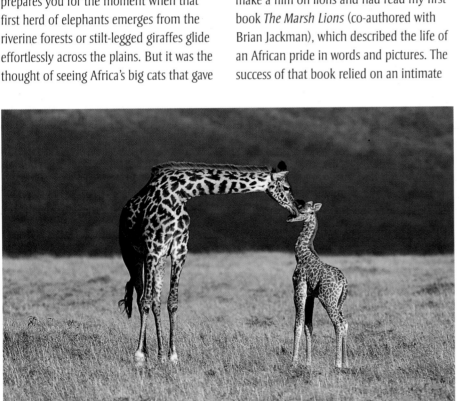

The Masai giraffe is found in southern Kenya and Tanzania, and is one of three East African subspecies.

drivers and guides working at the tented camps and lodges scattered in and around the reserve, we have followed some of these cats since they were born, and others until they died. Such an intimate relationship with wild animals is possible only when they feel totally relaxed in your presence. That's the challenge. Though the lions, leopards and cheetahs don't recognize us as individuals, they do get used to being watched on a daily basis and are much more relaxed if approached cautiously. Lion cubs in the Mara hear the sound of a vehicle before their eyes have even opened, and because their mothers have been raised within view of tourists and generally ignore their presence, young cubs quickly learn to do the same. The ease with which all three big cats can be approached in the Musiara area was one of the main reasons for choosing it as the location for *Big Cat Diary*.

The idea for the series came from Keith Scholey (now head of the BBC Natural History Unit) and reflected radical changes that swept through the wildlife film-making industry in the mid-1990s. Suddenly presenter-led wildlife programmes and fly-

on-the-wall documentaries (often filmed with the help of the new generation of small, easy-to-use digital video – dv – cameras) were much in demand. In-depth investigations into the social life of lions or wild dogs – the 'blue chip' productions taking two years to film and consuming large sums of money – had begun to lose their appeal with the programme controllers. Angie and I had the opportunity to experience the new way of doing things when we were asked to work as presenters on an American television programme called *Wild Things*. That series followed the lives of wildlife biologists, photographers, vets and animal-capture teams as they went about their daily business. It relied heavily on situations guaranteeing plenty of action, with presenters very much to the fore – 'actuality' became the new buzzword. *Wild Things* ran for three years with camera crews covering locations in more than 40 countries. It was a hands-on, warts-and-all approach – no tripods, no narration, just the participants talking directly to camera. There was a tremendous energy to this style of filming, and a lot of fun, too. The

programmes seemed to mirror what today's audiences wanted, with the focus as much on immediacy and entertainment as on animal behaviour. The old, more formal style of presentation was out as far as mainstream television was concerned.

There is no doubting the appeal of this kind of show, but there are risks too, not least the danger of trivializing the lives of the animals being filmed. *Big Cat Diary* took a more cautious approach while embracing some of these changes. We all realized that the demand for more and more action could be highly damaging, encouraging a tendency to disturb the animals unnecessarily in the remorseless quest for new and exciting shots. It also sometimes creates a false sense of how the animals really live. For every action sequence shot in the wild there are usually many hours of sitting and waiting, when nothing much is happening because the lions or leopards are asleep – something all big cats do for most of the day and night. Of course, nobody wants to watch lions dozing for long, particularly a TV audience with access to numerous alternatives at the click of a button. But I sometimes feel that wildlife programmes are regressing to a 'nature red in tooth and claw' approach, with everything having to appear big, bad and dangerous simply to hold people's attention. It's as if the animals weren't interesting and exciting enough in their own right. In the process we risk destroying our natural sense of wonder at the extraordinary diversity and splendour of life on our planet.

When the first series of *Big Cat Diary* was filmed six years ago, it soon became apparent that with all the resources at our disposal we could almost guarantee plenty of dramatic images. With five camera crews and a number of game-spotters searching for the big cats from dawn to dusk each day, it was tempting to revert to the old style of programme-making, letting the wildlife footage lead the way. The idea of including life in camp and daily mishaps

Wild dogs are the second most endangered large carnivore in Africa, with between 3,000 and 5,000 remaining (there are fewer than 500 Ethiopian wolves).

Impalas are common in the Mara; they are a favourite prey of leopards and wild dogs, and an important part of the diet of lions in some areas.

was quickly abandoned, as was the plan occasionally to use cameramen as presenters. In that first series, Simon and I were invariably seen talking to the audience from the windows of our vehicles, presenting in a more formal way. Four years later, for the third series, a dv cameraman accompanied Simon and me at all times to try and capture the sense of intimacy that we share with the big cats and increase the audience's involvement with what we were witnessing. The viewers were able to connect to the way we were feeling, instead of just listening to facts and figures about what was happening. Now there was some real emotion to the day-to-day events, with a genuine sense of 'live' television, even though the programmes were transmitted at a later date.

One of the frustrations of television is that there is so little time to share information with the audience. There's always another strand to an animal's story, background material that could provide a more detailed picture of its life. If only there was time to tell it. But this is simply not possible in a 30-minute programme. So when Angie and I proposed the idea of writing a book to accompany the fourth series of *Big Cat Diary* we had in mind a 'companion' volume to the series. This

would help to provide a historical perspective to the Masai Mara and its big cats, detailing the lives of some of the animal characters with whom the audience had identified over the last six years – the leopards Half-Tail and her daughter Shadow (known to the local drivers as Zawadi, meaning 'gift'), the Marsh Lions and Amber the cheetah. It was a relief when our publishers suggested individual titles on each of the big cats, starting with lions, rather than the single publication we had envisaged. There were just too many questions to try to answer, and more than anything we wanted to give a sense of the bigger picture, to explore the way in which each of the big cats copes with life not only in the Mara but in other parts of Africa. We also wanted to examine what could be done to try and ensure their survival.

Angie and I have always believed that Kenya's Masai Mara and Tanzania's Serengeti and Ngorongoro Crater represent the best big-cat game-viewing country in Africa. Certainly there can be few places where they are more visible. But Zimbabwe, Zambia, Botswana, Namibia and South Africa all have areas where lions, leopards and cheetahs survive in healthy populations. Last year we visited the better-known wildlife sanctuaries in these

countries to catch up with the latest research on big cats and discover the best places to see them. We are often asked to name our favourite big cat destinations, and for that reason have included a brief travel section at the end of the book, together with a list of websites concerned with big cat conservation.

Sitting and watching a recording of *Big Cat Diary* in England recently, we realized how easy it would be to imagine that all was well in the world of the lion; that the threat posed by the trade in spotted coats had diminished to such a degree that the leopard was no longer endangered in certain parts of the world; and that the graceful cheetah was holding its own despite all the problems faced by this least adaptable of big cats. Yet the Masai Mara Reserve is only 1510 km² (600sq. miles) in extent and is surrounded on three sides by a burgeoning human population. Only to the south, in the vastness of the adjoining Serengeti National Park, are there still large tracts of land where the animals can wander freely. And even there wildlife is increasingly threatened by man's impact, whether in the form of wire snares set by illegal meat hunters or by pressure to develop the surrounding land for agriculture. Where once wild animals

Plains zebras in Moremi Game Reserve, Okavango Delta, Botswana. The Okavango is a superb place for big cats, with large prides of lions and a good chance of seeing leopards, cheetahs – and wild dogs.

roamed across much of Africa, they now live in islands among a sea of humanity.

Despite the obvious pressures, however, the Mara is still a place to be marvelled at. It is part of Masailand, held in trust by the Kenyan government and administered by the local county councils on behalf of the Masai people. Some of the revenue from visitors' park entrance fees is ploughed back into the local community in the form of schools and dispensaries. Though the *Big Cat Diary* camp is situated inside the reserve, a lot of filming takes place beyond the boundary, where Amber the cheetah spends much of her time, where Half-Tail the leopard lived before her untimely death and where we now search for Shadow. The land bordering the reserve is divided into large group ranches, a form of communal land ownership. Visitors who stay in safari camps or lodges in this area now pay their fees directly to representatives of the local community rather than to the county council. But the average Masai herdsman protests that he still sees little return from tolerating the presence of wildlife on his land, and that it is only the government, tour operators and owners of tented camps and lodges who make a tidy profit.

In the 25 years that I have been living and working in the Mara the inevitable changes have gathered pace. The group ranches are being subdivided so as to give individual title to landowners. Nobody could argue with that and it should be a straightforward process, a Masai affair. But title to some of the land is being given to outsiders, breeding discontent among the rightful owners. The worry is that Masailand will eventually disappear under a patchwork of fences and agriculture (in places it already has), instead of large tracts of land being preserved as valuable wildlife habitat, which if managed properly could generate far more income for the owners than agriculture or cattle.

One of the dilemmas faced by *Big Cat Diary* has always been how much we should show of the lives of the Masai people in order to provide a better sense of place. The same applies to the question of whether or not to include shots of visitors on safari: pristine as it might look on a television screen, the Mara receives upwards of 250,000 visitors a year. There is no question that Africa desperately needs the revenue from tourism to help pay for conservation, but it comes at a cost to the environment. But the BBC Natural History Unit is in the business of making natural history programmes, not social commentary. When Half-Tail was presumed to have been killed in a wire snare after a stock-raiding incident, however, we were given the opportunity to present some of the issues, looking at the story both from a conservationist's point of view and from the grass-roots reality of being a livestock owner living among large predators.

You can't separate the fate of the animals from human destiny. 'Progress' is riding roughshod over the aspirations of nomadic peoples across the world. Their itinerant lifestyle always guaranteed that they would be the last to be drawn into the cash economy, clinging to their ancient customs as they tried to find a way to shape a future from their past. Today the issue of land rights has great significance for the Aboriginal people of Australia and the native peoples of North America, as it does for the Kalahari Bushmen and the Masai of Africa. So too does it have significance for the wild creatures. Lions, leopards and cheetahs need vast tracts of wilderness if they are to survive. As Paul Funston, a biologist studying lions in the Kalahari, said, 'The future of wildlife conservation in Africa rests on negotiating an agreement between people and parks.'

Only with the goodwill of the local people, fuelled by equitable distribution of profits, can this happen. If it does there is a chance that the land of the lion will survive.

Half-Tail and her daughter Shadow. A leopard mother is ever watchful for lions and hyenas who might endanger the life of her cubs or steal her food.

# King of Beasts

Our fascination with big cats – all cats – is ancient and universal: we admire their sleek beauty, the graceful way they move, and watch spellbound when suddenly they crouch, ready to pounce. Beholding a lion at that moment, we feel an atavistic connection with the hunter, the age-old mixture of wonder and fear – wonder at the beauty tempered by the fear of one day finding ourselves the focus of its predatory intentions. It seems only fitting to begin this series of books celebrating Africa's big cats with the lion. They are after all the creature visitors most want to see on safari, embodying the primordial spirit of savanna Africa. They are the king of beasts.

Nobody is sure how many lions are left in the wild. But we do know that they are increasingly under threat throughout their range. Many people feel that there is no place for wild lions in today's world, especially when so many of Africa's people are faced with unimaginable poverty: 40 per cent live on less than one dollar a day. When a lion kills a cow it is a huge loss to its owners. The lion becomes man's enemy and is pursued and destroyed. Should we be surprised when the Masai herdsman picks up his spear to protect his property, even his life? If we are to ensure the lion's survival, we must find a way of dealing with this dilemma.

To understand man's response to predators we need to examine our past. It isn't by chance that the lion has achieved such a hold over the human psyche. Lions seem such a quintessential part of the African landscape that it is easy to forget that not so long ago they roamed vast areas of the world, and in prehistoric times must have numbered in their millions. Today there are probably 30,000 at most, with fewer and fewer lions able to find sufficient food outside protected areas without coming into conflict with man and his livestock.

For millions of years some form of big cat has dominated the predator hierarchy across the globe. By the time our primate relatives abandoned the forests and a largely vegetarian diet to gather food and hunt out on the savannas of Africa, that cat was a lion. The lion was everything that we were not: a huge, immensely powerful

Male lions measure up to 3.3m (11ft), including a tail of up to 1m (3.3ft) and stand 1.2m (4ft) at the shoulder.

The demise of dinosaurs such as *Tyrannosaurus rex* 65 million years ago opened the door for a surge in mammalian evolution.

creature able to kill with a single swipe of its paw or a crushing bite from its fearsome canines. How we must have feared it - and no wonder we revere it. The evolution of our own social behaviour has been moulded to some degree by competition with predators, particularly lions. Certainly our early ancestors would have needed to know something about the way lions lived – if for no other reason than to try and prevent themselves from being eaten. Only by co-operating could we have outwitted animals as formidable as lions.

To trace the history of the evolution of these great carnivores you have to travel back in time. Some 65 million years ago (65 mya), when giant reptiles ruled the world (they had been the dominant predators for nearly 150 million years), small insectivorous creatures the size of a squirrel, with long pointed faces and cusped teeth, busied themselves among the prehistoric undergrowth of the northern hemisphere. These early mammals were shrew-like creatures with short flexible limbs, and they showed the first signs of development of cheek teeth, whose scissor-like action for cutting through skin and flesh allowed them to supplement their diet of insects with the occasional small vertebrate.

With the demise of the dinosaurs came a surge in mammalian evolution. From the beginning predators and prey evolved in tandem. Two separate lineages of meat-eaters emerged. One, comprising animals known as miacids, gave rise to the order Carnivora, which divided into two distinct branches, one representing the cat-like species (cats, genets, civets and mongooses) and the other the bear- and dog-like species, and the seals. The other group were members of the archaic order Creodonta (meaning 'flesh-tooth'), small-brained creatures with 44 teeth, long bodies, short legs and clawed toes. They were plantigrade – walking on the soles of their feet – and the first digit on their forefeet could be opposed to the others, like those of modern primates or like a human thumb, suggesting that they possessed the ability to grasp branches and climb. The creodonts flourished from about 55–35 mya and were the dominant meat-eaters at this time. They ranged through North America, Eurasia and Africa, rapidly evolving into numerous and sometimes gigantic forms. But by 20–30 mya members of the Carnivora had assumed the position of top predators on the northern continents, and the last creodonts finally disappeared about 8 mya.

The early miacids were smaller than the creodonts, mongoose- or weasel-like creatures with wide paws and spreading digits with retractile claws for grasping. They were also distinguishable from the creodonts by the position in the jaw of their specialized scissor-like cheek teeth or carnassials. The creodonts' carnassials were formed from the rearmost teeth in the jaw, so they could eat only meat. But the carnassials of miacids were situated further forward, allowing them to use their back teeth for grinding up fibrous material such as fruit and vegetables. This greater flexibility in diet may have been the reason why the miacids eventually eclipsed the creodonts. As the earth became cooler and the climate more seasonal over the next few million years, there was a loss of plant diversity, which would have caused the creodonts' prey to become scarcer, while fruit and insects became seasonally more abundant, favouring the miacids.

Miacids hunted their prey in trees or dense undergrowth, and the burst of diversification at this time mirrored the proliferation in their prey. Modern viverrids – the genets and civet cats – have ten teeth in each jaw, 40 in all, and most closely resemble the ancestral miacids, though as a family they show greater diversity than either the cats or the hyenas. Jonathan Kingdon, an expert on the evolution of African mammals says, '....it is possible to regard the palm civet as the contemporary equivalent of an arboreal miacid, while the genets and civets represent arboreal and terrestrial offshoots. So cat-like is the genet that we can easily envisage the

All members of the order Carnivora are distinguished by the scissor-like cheek teeth, known as carnassials, that allow them to cut through skin and flesh.

development of felids from such creatures.' Modern hyenas developed directly from an ancestral viverrid that would have borne some resemblance to the living civet, and they share certain features with cats, such as the reduction in number of teeth and modifications to the middle ear, hinting at a common ancestor. Among the carnivores there is only one family whose members are all specialized killers: the cats.

About 40 mya a number of cat-like forms appear in the fossil record of Europe and North America. They were initially thought to be ancestors of the true cats, hence their name Palaeofelids, meaning first or ancient cat. But these creatures are sufficiently different from modern cats – the Neofelids – to be considered a separate family, the Nimravidae, which evolved alongside the earliest ancestors of the true cats in a process known as convergent or parallel evolution. Both had long limbs, clawed feet, short faces and well-developed

carnassial teeth. Most of the Nimravidae had enormously long, flattened, blade-like upper canines – the 'sabre teeth' so loved by children and the producers of scary movies depicting prehistoric times. Despite their outlandish appearance, the Nimravidae were a successful family and became extinct only around 6 mya. In fact sabre teeth evolved independently on three different continents in at least four mammal groups, some of which were relatively small. The first sabre-toothed creature was a creodont by the name of *Machaeroides*, a powerful little animal somewhat like a genet that evolved 48 mya. Sabre-toothed forms evolved among the Neofelids, too, as early as 15 mya.

The earliest remains of a true cat come from France and date back to around 30 mya. They belong to *Proailurus lemanensis*, a smallish animal, similar to the fossa of Madagascar, a viverrid. Some 20 mya, a group of cats belonging to the genus *Pseudaelurus* emerged – they were the size of a large lynx or small mountain lion, and had much in common with modern cats. Two lines are evident among this group, one of which produced the sabre-toothed

species among the Neofelids. These included the famous American sabre-toothed cats of the genus *Smilodon* ('knife tooth'), which evolved about 2 mya. The largest of these was *Smilodon populator*, which was about the size of a modern-day lion with 17cm (7in) blade-like canines with finely serrated edges.

*Smilodon* had a massively powerful upper body and front limbs with large retractile claws adapted to hold on to its prey. It had a short tail like a lynx, so it may not have been particularly swift, possibly relying on ambush and stalking rather than speed in the chase to prey on juvenile mega-herbivores such as mammoths and rhino-like pachyderms. A short rush culminating in a bone-jarring collision with its hefty prey was probably the norm, with *Smilodon* relying on brute strength to pull its victim to a halt, anchoring it with meat-hook claws. *Smilodon* probably targeted soft, vascular areas such as the abdomen or throat. A bite to the neck would have risked hitting bone and shattering its long sabres.

Nobody is sure why sabre-toothed cats became extinct, though 5 or 6 mya climatic changes were already accelerating the

Though rather dog-like in appearance, spotted hyenas are more closely related to cats, with affinities to mongooses.

replacement of forests by more open habitats, which in turn led to the emergence of rodents and a profusion of antelopes and gazelles: fleet-footed prey that were too agile for sabre-toothed cats to hunt. This development saw the rise of the pantherine cats, which relied on both power and speed. They had no need for sabre-like teeth to kill and eat their soft-skinned prey, though for a while both kinds of cats lived side by side, each targeting its own victims. But the first human artists who etched the images of wild animals on the walls of their caves 35,000 years ago left no sign of sabre-toothed cats, and most had become extinct by then. It's probably no coincidence that as the large ungulates and thick-skinned mammoths and rhinoceroses became scarce towards the end of the Pleistocene epoch 10,000 years ago, the last of the sabre-toothed cats vanished with them.

The earliest known pantherine cat with lion-like attributes dates back to around 3.5 mya. It was found in Laetoli in Tanzania, where Mary Leakey and her co-workers discovered man's earliest footprints from about the same time. Surprisingly, considering their size, we have no fossil evidence for lions earlier than this, nor a likely ancestor, though the lion is thought to have emerged more recently than other members of the genus *Panthera*. Newly developed molecular techniques indicate that all modern lions probably shared a common ancestor perhaps as recently as 55,000–200,000 years ago.

The earliest records for true lions come from West Africa and date back to around 750,000 years ago. From here they spread north into Asia and Europe, and the oldest finds date to around 700,000 years ago at the Italian site of Isernia. The 'cave lion' (*Panthera spelaea*), as it became known, was widely distributed and its remains have been discovered in the river deposits and caves of England, Spain, France, Germany, Italy and Switzerland. Cave lions were enormous, thickset animals – probably the largest felid that ever lived. They were up to 25 per cent bigger than today's lions and are thought to have preyed on horses and deer, perhaps even some of the larger species of bovids. These Old World lions existed at the same time as the big Ice Age cat *Panthera atrox* roamed the Americas alongside *Smilodon*. The cave lions were similar enough to the modern lion, *Panthera leo*, for some authorities to consider them a subspecies, *Panthera leo spelaea*. Over time they became smaller until they were no more than 10 per cent bigger than modern lions and possessed a mane and tail tuft, something the earlier larger specimens lacked.

*Panthera atrox* shares many similarities with cave lions and it is quite possible that they were both subspecies of modern lions, rather than distinct species. Cats similar to cave lions are known from China and eastern Siberia, and some people think that lions living in the Balkans and Turkey as recently as 300BC were cave lions. The North American lion occurred throughout Alaska, while cave lions have been found in late Pleistocene deposits in eastern Siberia, close to the Bering Straits. During the last 40,000 years or so a land bridge has connected the two landmasses on more than one occasion. In fact some of the lion specimens found in Alaska are now thought to be more similar to cave lions than to North American lions, adding weight to the idea that they were closely related or even the same animal. Perhaps it is only the later and geographically more distinct populations of the North American lion that diverged sufficiently from the cave lion to warrant a different name. The North American lion survived as late as 11,600 years ago, by which time human occupation had already occurred, and is thought to have been a social species, forming groups or prides like today's lions.

Whether as a single species or a number

*Smilodon* in action: an artist's impression of a scene at Rancho La Brea, California, one of the world's richest fossil sites.

of subspecies it is evident that the lion had the greatest distribution of any terrestrial mammal. As recently as 10,000 years ago lions still spanned vast sections of the globe, from southern Europe eastwards through India and throughout the whole of the African continent except for the driest deserts and the rainforests. The last cave lions disappeared in Europe some time between 340BC and AD100, but the Asiatic lion *Panthera leo persica* – a subspecies that split from African lions some 100,000 years ago – clung on in Palestine until the Crusades. It survived well into the 20th Century in Syria and Iraq, and was reported in Iran in the 1940s. Some 200 years ago the Asiatic lion was still widely distributed over the northern half of the Indian subcontinent. But today the only wild lions outside Africa are some 300 Asiatic lions in the 1,400km² (560sq. mile) Gir Forest sanctuary of Gujarat State in India.

As with the eventual demise of the sabre-tooths, nobody is sure what caused lions to disappear from so much of their former range. The changing climate would surely have played its part, and the resulting shifts in vegetation patterns may have altered the type and abundance of prey available to lions. The fact that forests spread across much of Europe after the Ice Age may well have helped to hasten the retreat of a cat perhaps suited to more open terrain. Certainly competition with man would have been significant. Lions were the most dangerous animals with which our forebears had to contend and lions sometimes hunted and killed humans, as did leopards and sabre-toothed cats. The skulls of early humans have been recovered from their dens, crushed like egg shells by the big cats' powerful canines. But all that changed soon enough. What we lacked in strength and speed we made up for in foresight. Our large primate brain enabled us to learn how to hunt co-operatively and to scavenge kills from other predators. With the development of language we could communicate more efficiently; weapons

were refined. Now we could plan our attack on predator and prey, and had the weapons to do the killing.

Before long the physically weakest among the predators reigned supreme as small numbers of our ancestors left Africa 100,000 years ago to colonize the world, leaving a wave of destruction in their wake. Even so, man had still not achieved full domination of lions as recently as 25,000 years ago: Stone Age man was probably at best co-dominant with lions among the predators. But the advent of agriculture and the domestication of livestock signalled the beginning of the end for top predators such as the lion and wolf. With his livelihood to protect, man pursued predators with a vengeance, and later the development of firearms as much as anything else hastened the demise of the world's large predators. The natural prey species of the wolf and the lion soon began to disappear in a hail of bullets, and with them went the animals that fed on them. By the beginning of the 20th Century the black-maned Cape lion, *Panthera leo melanochaita*, had vanished from its stronghold in the southernmost reaches of the continent, and by the 1930s the last remaining North African or Barbary lions, *Panthera leo Leo*, with their magnificent dark manes extending behind their shoulders and covering their bellies, had vanished from their final retreat in Morocco's rugged Atlas Mountains, although they lingered for a while in royal palaces and zoos.

Between 1800 and the early 1900s, man slaughtered wild animals on a colossal scale, fuelled by greed and a lack of concern for the consequences. Up to 60 million bison were wiped out across the length and breadth of North America, destroying the Native Americans' way of life and opening up the land to cattle. By 1903 there were just 21 wild buffalo left and the haunting cry of the wolf came to symbolize the loss of wilderness – a poignant and

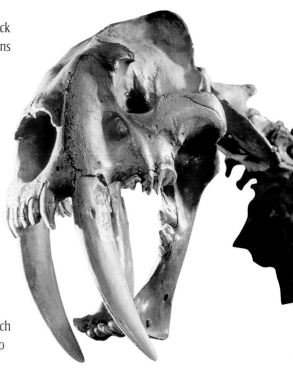

The largest species of *Smilodon* was lion-sized with sabre teeth of up to 28cm (11in), of which 17cm (6¾in) protruded from the upper jaw.

melancholy sound.

The Great Slaughter, as Colin Willock describes it in his book *Wildfight: A History of Conservation*, wasn't limited to the American continent. Before the arrival of European settlers in southern Africa, huge numbers of dainty springboks, blue wildebeest and zebra-like quaggas migrated seasonally over vast areas, just as Thomson's gazelles, white-bearded wildebeest and plains zebras do today in the Serengeti and the Masai Mara. Then came the farmers and hide-hunters. In 1836, 7,000 hardy Afrikaners abandoned the Cape Colony for what were to become the Orange Free State, Natal and the Transvaal. The exodus was prompted by their search for a land free of British rule. Under pressure from Parliament and public opinion in England, in 1828 the Cape authorities had decreed that free natives had the same rights and protection as settlers. Five years later the Slave Emancipation Act ended slavery throughout the British Empire – a quarter of the world – and required that 36,000 slaves in Cape

The migration numbers 1.3 million wildebeest and 200,000 zebras, with some 350,000 Thomson's gazelles moving over a more restricted area.

Colony should be set free by 1838. The Boers saw equality as a loss of their own rights, emancipation as theft of their property. Boer scouting parties had already found fertile land north of the Orange River, rich with game and virtually unpopulated. The Voortrekkers, Bible in one hand and rifle in the other, loaded their families and meagre possessions onto ox wagons, and took their slaves with them. Many were crack shots, as the British found to their cost during the Boer War. But above all they were farmers through and through, and they loved to hunt.

People estimate that in those days 40 million springboks roamed large parts of southern Africa, and vast numbers of them migrated from the interior to escape times of drought. Today's greatest wildlife spectacle – the Serengeti–Mara's 1.3 million wildebeest, 350,000 gazelles and 200,000 zebras – pales by comparison. The springboks would gather in huge concentrations wherever scattered thunderstorms created a green flush, only to vanish again as soon as rain began to fall in the interior. Like the nomadic wildebeest, they could sense the rainfall from far away. The Voortrekkers viewed the primarily grass-eating springboks as if they were a plague of rabbits, competitors to their livestock and a source of saleable hides and the dried meat known as biltong.

The Scottish hunter and adventurer George Gordon Cumming describes a typical scene during a springbok migration or *trekbokken* in 1844.

*Looking about me I beheld the ground to the northward of my camp actually covered by a dense living mass of springboks, marching slowly and steadily along and extending from an opening in a long range of hills to the west, through which they continued pouring like the flood of some great river, about a mile to the north-east over which they disappeared. The breadth of the ground they covered might have been somewhere about half a mile. I stood upon the fore-chest of my wagon for about two hours… During this time, vast legions continued streaming through the neck of the hills in one unbroken compact phalanx.*

The awe that Cumming and his men felt did not deter them from riding into the herd and dispatching 14 of them.

Little wonder, then, that the quagga disappeared forever in 1883, not on the southern African veldt whose wide plains had once been darkened for as far as the eye could see with a moving phalanx of wildebeest and quaggas. The solitary survivor of the race died in a cage in the Amsterdam Zoo.

Even when game sanctuaries were created to protect a remnant of wildlife for posterity, predators were viewed with suspicion, particularly the lion – predator of man and beast. The most damaging accusation levelled against creatures such as lions was that unless vigorously kept in check they would decimate the prey populations (the irony being that man was already doing that himself). Sympathy rested with the doe-eyed quarry rather than the hunting animal. The beautiful antelope must be protected from the rapacious lion. Particular scorn was reserved for wild dogs and hyenas, hunters that chased their prey to exhaustion before pulling it apart. Their method of killing by disembowelment was seen as 'unsporting' – not just by farmers, but by hunters and game wardens alike. At the end of the 19th Century there were an estimated 200,000 wild dogs in Africa. Today there are 5,000 at most, possibly only 3,000. The big cats were thought of in a somewhat different light, partly due to the way they dispatched their prey with a single killing bite. But man has always struggled to view predators as anything other than competitors, and they were still classed as vermin. Even the mild-mannered cheetahs felt the brunt of this anti-predator sentiment and they were killed in their hundreds.

Fortunately there were always some enlightened individuals struggling to stem the tide. One such was James Stevenson-Hamilton, who in 1902 was appointed first warden of South Africa's Sabi Game Reserve. This was a monumental achievement considering the attitude of the general populace. Stevenson-Hamilton's brief was to 'make myself as unpopular as possible among hunters and poachers'. He believed that nature was the best manager of wildlife and if left alone would balance the numbers of predators and prey, sentiments that were years ahead of their time. But residents of the Lowveld bordering the park were reluctant to accept that the aims of the sanctuary were to eliminate the influence of modern man and to preserve all wildlife – predators and their prey. Matters were complicated by the fact that uncontrolled killing of game, both inside and outside the reserve, for meat, hides and trophies had prompted the lions to turn to stock-raiding. Under the circumstances Stevenson-Hamilton reluctantly agreed to reduce the number of lions until the prey animals recovered, though he was the first to admit that the predators 'kill off all the old and weak stock among the game and so allow the fittest to survive'.

Despite Stevenson-Hamilton's efforts to keep carnivore control within reasonable limits, between 1903 and 1927 the minimum number of predators killed by the warden and his staff was: 1,272 lions, 660 leopards, 269 cheetahs, 521 hyenas, 1,142 wild dogs and 635 crocodiles. When the smaller predators, reptiles and birds of prey were included the total came to 18,428 animals. But by 1926 ideas had progressed to the point that the sanctuary could be opened up to sightseeing and nature photography, heralding the advent of tourism, and Shingwidzi and Sabi Game Reserves were proclaimed as Africa's first national park, the Kruger.

It soon became apparent that the animals people wanted to see most were the big cats – particularly lions – followed by elephants and giraffes. In his last annual report in 1945 Stevenson-Hamilton estimated the number of adult lions in the park to be about 800; when he took charge of the Sabi area in 1902 there had been just nine. By the 1950s scientific research had begun to become part of the management of the park and concerns over the legitimacy of culling predators to protect the prey animals were being taken seriously. Nonetheless 51 cheetahs were killed between 1954 and 1960. Finally, in 1960, carnivore control was officially abandoned. Even so, it is estimated that a minimum of 4,000 Kruger Park lions were killed between 1902 and 1969.

A nomadic male lion strangling a warthog. Lions employ a single killing bite that incapacitates their prey quickly.

East Africa still favours the ban on ivory trading, while most
southern African countries would like to see the market opened
up: in the past the trade has helped them to fund conservation.

nomadic Masai and itinerant Waikoma who hunted with poisoned arrows and game pits during the dry season. The only semi-permanent residents were Wandorobo hunters who slept in caves in the central ranges and traded meat and skins with the Waikoma in return for sheep. To the north-east the Loita Hills formed an unknown barrier to early explorers and hunters from Kenya, who were unable to persuade the Masai to guide them any further south. And in the north in the Ikoma region the sleeping sickness belt barred their way.

However, once the discovery had been made, tranquillity did not last long for the wild animals. Kenya, as much as any country in Africa, can claim to be the birthplace of safaris – hunting safaris – a tradition dating back to the beginning of the 19th Century, when hardy settlers supplemented their income by taking out visiting sportsmen in search of big game. Even before the railroad reached Nairobi in 1900, porters and ox carts were venturing into the hinterland from the coast, and with the ending of the First World War hunters began to open up the Serengeti to vehicles.

Sport hunting was a long-cherished tradition in England, just as it was on the European continent and in North America. Not that there was much 'sport' about some of the hunting. The object of one Serengeti safari was to shoot lions with bows and arrows, backed up by men in cars armed with rifles. Within the space of three months, 51 lions were shot, though only five were killed by bow and arrow, one of them a lioness asleep in a tree.

From 1925 onwards the Serengeti was *the* place to shoot lions. One hunter describes how: 'After a light breakfast we dashed off in a fast car to see how many lions we could select for rugs.' They finished off their safari by bringing in a party of Nandi spearmen from Kenya who speared four lions for their film. By now the killing had reached such proportions that the Tanganyika government proclaimed a 2,300km² (900sq. mile) lion sanctuary in

The Masai Mara and Serengeti, where big cats can still be found in large numbers and which boast a combined population of 3,000 lions, remained unknown to Europeans until little more than a hundred years ago. In those days much of the Masai Mara was heavily wooded (the name Mara means 'spotted' in the Masai language) – it was a land stippled with acacia woodland and swarming with tsetse flies, which transmit a form of sleeping sickness deadly to cattle. The German explorer Oscar Baumann was probably the first European to see the Serengeti plains when he travelled westwards from Ngorongoro Crater in 1892. There are good reasons why it took so long for the settlers to explore this part of Masailand. Even the 'slavers' avoided the Serengeti area, which was considered fever-ridden country with miles of low bush and little water. It was an uninhabited game area, home to a few

the heart of the Serengeti. But the killing of lions continued unabated around the borders of the sanctuary until 1937, when all hunting was stopped and the Serengeti became a permanent game reserve.

North of the border, in Kenya, the story of destruction had a familiar ring to it. The Mara region was opened up to hunting after the Second World War and for a while there was uncontrolled slaughter for trophies and biltong. Fires set by poachers and honey hunters penetrated the Mara's dense stands of acacia bush, allowing grasslands to take hold and enabling the Masai to return with their cattle. In 1948, a 520km² (200sq. mile) area between the Siria Escarpment, the Tanzanian border and the Mara River (today known as the Mara Triangle) was declared a national game reserve and hunting was regulated. In 1961 the reserve came under the direct control of the Narok County Council and its borders

Impalas can leap 10ft (3m) into the air and 30ft (9m) in breadth, helping them to avoid the clutches of a predator and make good their escape.

were extended east of the river to include the area where *Big Cat Diary* is now filmed. But borders are never absolute in today's world. Three sections were excised in 1984 to give the Masai and their livestock access to dry-season watering points and the reserve was brought to its present size of 1510km² (600sq. miles), representing a loss of 10 per cent of the area set aside for wildlife. Today more than ever the Masai covet the rich grazing land within the reserve.

Moru Kopjes, in Serengeti, are a spectacular collection of ancient granite rock forms. Some of the rocks near Seronera, in the centre of the park, are among the oldest on earth – two to three billion years old.

# Living with the Pride

Surprisingly little was known about lions, leopards or cheetahs until the American biologist George Schaller completed his three-year study of Africa's large predators in the Serengeti in 1969. Before that animal behaviour was generally viewed in an anthropomorphic vein, coloured by the myths and anecdotes of the early explorers and hunters. Their accounts were more often concerned with how many lions or rhinos they had killed in a day and how easy the hunting was, rather than providing insights into the way animals lived. Studies made in zoos often proved misleading, particularly with regard to the more social creatures. It wasn't until the late 1950s that biologists began to leave the laboratory to study animals in the field, and when they did a whole new world of complexity emerged. Schaller logged 149,000km (93,125 miles) in pursuit of his subjects in a block of about 650km² (250sq. miles) around Seronera in the centre of the park, and spent 2,900 hours observing lions. The time had come to separate fact from fiction and to give the world a new creature – the Serengeti lion.

While George Schaller was busy studying lions in the Serengeti, a remarkable Hungarian woman called Judith Rudnai set to work exploring the habits and ecology of the lions in the Nairobi National Park for her Masters degree. Her brief was to provide the authorities with solid information on the park's number-one tourist attraction. She was particular keen to discover what effect lion predation was having on prey populations, the same question that John Owen, then Director of Tanzania National Parks, had asked George Schaller to answer in the Serengeti. Until now, people had presumed that the answer was too obvious to need verifying – predators were by their very nature detrimental to prey populations and, if protected, lions, cheetahs, hyenas and wild dogs would overrun large areas and play havoc with the game. Given time, scientists such as Schaller and Rudnai would prove

Dr Scott Creel (left) and Goran Spong fit a radio-collar and take blood samples from a lioness in the Selous Game Reserve, Tanzania.

Each lion has a unique pattern of whisker spots, as individual as human fingerprints, which remain the same throughout its life.

just how wrong and destructive these assumptions had been.

The contrasts between Schaller and Rudnai's studies were enormous, the only common thread being the lions. Rudnai was working within sight and sound of a capital city of a million inhabitants (it has now grown to three million), in a park of only 117km² (45sq. miles), which was fenced on three sides, surrounded by urban sprawl and received 200,000 visitors a year. Not quite what one visualizes as wild Africa, despite its attractions. Meanwhile Schaller was roaming a park a hundred times larger, with no more than 50,000 visitors a year. But despite the differences in ambience it soon became apparent that certain basic tenets of lion behaviour held true.

People had already deduced that lions were the exception among the cat family in being social, with adult males and females living together in groups known as prides. Both Schaller and Rudnai realized that the key to studying social animals lay in being able to identify individuals. While Schaller relied on radio collars and ear tags to help him track and identify his study animals, this was not the answer for Rudnai. In the relatively small and confined area of Nairobi Park radio-collaring was unnecessary, and anyway the park authorities would never have agreed – visitors want their lions to look wild, and in a population of just 30 lions the collared ones would have been highly visible.

Instead, Rudnai devised a far more novel and less intrusive method. On either side of its muzzle, every lion has rows of long whiskers known as vibrissae, which help it to feel its way around in the dark. Each tuft of whiskers emanates from a dark spot. Rudnai had noticed that one of the lionesses she was watching had a crooked line of spots on one side of her face, making it easy to recognize her. This prompted her to test if every lion had a different pattern of spots, rather as all humans have different fingerprints. With the help of her study supervisor Laurence Pennyquick she put her hunch to the test. It turned out that not only did every lion have a different pattern of spot markings, but that the pattern remained the same throughout life.

Soon anyone studying lions was using the whisker-spot method to identify them. By taking photographs of either side of a lion's face and of the front, it's possible to construct a 'mug shot' of each individual, adding ear notches and the pattern of spots on the nose for good measure. As a lion ages its nose changes from being totally pink to having a number of black spots which gradually coalesce. Rudnai's method proved far more reliable than trying to identify a lion because it had only one eye or part of its tail missing. Such injuries and old battle scars are not uncommon – and given time even the most disfiguring wounds may heal without a trace. Manes may darken and body size change, making an animal appear totally different when you next see it, which may be years later.

Lions have always been characterized as lazy, partly because they sleep so much, spending most of the daylight hours slumped beneath a thornbush. But lions are just being lions, and they are primarily nocturnal animals. Once they have killed and feasted on a diet rich in protein they can afford to do very little until the next meal or until they next feel the urge to patrol their territory or link up with other members of their pride. With so little happening during daylight, both Schaller and Rudnai were given permission to follow the lions after dark. Rudnai loved the experience of tracking lions on a moonlit night and in those days everyone was free

to drive off-road in Nairobi Park. In the cool of the night the lions transformed into very different kinds of animals, though they still spent much of the time resting.

During the first series of *Big Cat Diary* we too had a unique opportunity to observe big cats at night. Using infrared lights and cameras we were able to illuminate their world without unduly disturbing them (they are unable to see light of infrared wave length and so were not affected by it). Each morning I would cross paths with the night crew on their way back into camp, bleary-eyed and cold from the long chill nights. Sometimes they saw nothing and the lions (the main focus of their efforts) gave them the slip. But we tempered our sympathies in the knowledge that they were about to tuck into a cooked breakfast of mammoth proportions before showering and collapsing into bed. We always stopped for a brief chat, eager to know what they had seen in the hope that we could benefit from their sightings and relocate our quarry more easily. Having already viewed some of the footage, we marvelled at just how much of an advantage night-time bestowed on creatures such as lions and leopards.

The eyes of all cats are wonderfully adapted for night vision, and are six times more sensitive to light than man's. This is achieved in a number of ways. Cats have larger apertures (pupils) and lenses in proportion to their retinas (the light-sensitive layer of cells at the back of the eye) than humans, and a higher proportion of rods – the even more light-sensitive cells in the retina, best suited to night vision. Being a diurnal species, we have fewer rods and more cones – the cells designed to produce better vision in bright light. Cats also have an extra layer of cells behind the retina called the *tapetum lucidum*. This reflects any light back through the retina, allowing it a second chance at detecting it and transmitting the information to the brain.

Having such light-sensitive eyes poses the problem of how to protect them in

broad daylight. Anyone who has owned a domestic cat must have wondered at the slit-like appearance of its pupils during the day. When it is dark the pupils of the smaller species of cats enlarge and become almost circular, allowing the maximum of light to reach the retina. But during daylight a small cat's pupil can be closed to a slit by the action of the ciliary muscles, which are drawn across each other instead of being arranged in a circle around the pupil, as they are in our own eyes – and those of a lion. The advantage of a slit is that it can close the pupil down to a greater degree, and lets in less light than even the most condensed round pupil. Add to this the effect of partially closing the eyelids, and the amount of light entering the eye can be reduced even further.

Big cats, such as lions, leopards and cheetahs, do not have slit pupils – a lion's are only slightly oval in shape. This may be due to the fact that the smaller cats are generally more nocturnal than their larger relatives and may see even better than them in the dark. Cheetahs hunt almost exclusively in daylight, and leopards – particularly when they have cubs and must hunt more frequently or need to try and avoid competition with lions and hyenas – remain very opportunistic and often hunt during the day. Lions also hunt during the daytime when they are hungry, for instance by staking out a waterhole and ambushing prey that comes to drink in the middle of the day. Nevertheless most cats – big or small – are primarily nocturnal.

In the past I had never been able to spend much time following animals at night, and didn't have the benefit of night-vision binoculars on the rare occasion that I tried to. Using a vehicle's headlights and conventional spotlight tends to disturb the predators, and there is always the risk that one might endanger the prey by dazzling

Scar with one of Khali's ten-week-old cubs. Scar is the kind of lion that every visitor to Africa hopes to see.

Members of the Big Pride at dusk. Though the lion is certainly king among Africa's land predators, when a herd of elephants appears the lions tend – wisely – to give way.

them, giving the predator an unfair advantage to which they are quick to respond. But now the headlights of the night crew's vehicle were masked with infrared filters and an infrared camera mounted on the roof relayed a black and white image on to a small monitor positioned above the steering wheel, so that the driver could see where he was going.

On one occasion I had the opportunity of joining the night crew so that I could share with the audience the experience of filming at night. The moment I strapped on a pair of night-vision goggles the darkened world outside my window sprang to life. It wasn't like seeing in daylight – there was a greenish-yellow glow to whatever I looked at – but at least I could see. The problems started when I tried to move the vehicle. It felt a little like being in a moon buggy, with the world out there reduced to a 15x10cm (6x4in) black and white image. There was no sense of scale to what I was seeing, and it took time to adjust to how big and immovable those boulders really were or how deep was the drop-off that lay ahead of me. At times the repercussions were as damaging to the human anatomy as to the car.

Meanwhile the lions – when we could find them – walked across our monitor as if it was daylight, and it was quite apparent that they could see extremely well on even the darkest nights: the darker the better as far as hunting success was concerned. It might be pitch black to human eyes, but there were the lions ambling about with their young cubs scampering along besides them, picking a pathway through the rockiest terrain without faltering, as we stumbled and struggled to keep them in view. It was eerie to watch a lioness, seemingly exposed in the open without the benefit of cover, slinking across open ground in a semi-crouch towards a herd of wildebeest. Yet the wildebeest seemed blithely unaware of the predator's approach and just stood and stared. Until what? Did they hear the lioness's muffled footsteps first, or catch her musky scent, or finally pick up her movement from out of the darkness? Whatever the reason, prey quite often escaped due to their speed off the mark. I can only imagine that herbivores such as wildebeest, which need to spend most of the day and night feeding, don't possess such acute night vision as the primarily nocturnal cats.

Certainly it is far cooler for lions hunting at night. This is to their advantage, as they have very few sweat glands and must pant rapidly to cool down if they exert themselves unduly, synchronizing their panting to the rhythm of their breathing. You sometimes see a lion lying with no cover near at hand, panting at over 200 times a minute, sucking air into its mouth and over its tongue to evaporate moisture from the mucous membranes. This cools the blood and reduces the body temperature. Far better, then, to hunt at night, with the added benefit for prides living outside or on the fringes of the reserve of avoiding contact with the Masai, who retreat with their livestock inside their thornbush bomas as it begins to get dark.

Not only was it generally easier for the lions to catch prey at night, but the night crew were able to record lions hunting species that they would usually ignore during the day. On more than one occasion the lions took impalas and Grant's gazelles – a species that even the speedy cheetah and persistent wild dog find it hard to outrun – by sneaking up on them while they were lying down resting. Confused in the darkness, the antelopes were no match for four or five lionesses converging on them simultaneously. By co-operating in this way, the lions were able to achieve greater success in hunting these species than a single lioness on her own. But as Schaller and Rudnai discovered, the lionesses never seemed in any great hurry to hunt, as if they knew that something would eventually wander in their direction – and sooner or later it did. After an initial burst of activity in the early evening when they searched for prey, they often settled down again and slept for most of the night.

The night crew spent most of their time following a pride of lions known as the Big Pride, lions who had once been part of the Marsh Pride (the pride on which *Big Cat Diary* focuses) but had broken away some years earlier and now lived further to the north in the acacia country beyond the

*It soon became apparent that the process of regulating the number of females in a pride was actually taking place at the time we were filming the Big Pride. A subadult female of about two to three years of age was constantly bullied by the older females, particularly the ones with small cubs, forced to keep her distance for fear of being attacked. They no doubt viewed her as unwanted competition for food, especially now that they had another generation of young cubs to feed, irrespective of the fact that one of these females was probably the subadult's mother. The young female was old enough to hunt for herself, but she still persisted in trying to stay with the pride, constantly adopting submissive postures to ward off aggression. For the moment she seemed prepared to trail around after her older relatives whatever the cost. It was heart-rending to watch the way she was shunned by her pride mates, but almost inevitable that the young female would eventually be forced to become a nomad.*

The migration of wildebeest and zebras is the largest mammal migration on earth. At times, the wildebeest form a massed feeding front, chopping down the long red oat grass as they enter the Mara at the beginning of the dry season.

reserve boundary. There were eight lionesses in the pride, most of whom had small cubs. Lion society is built upon a tightly bonded sisterhood, an alliance of related females of various ages – sisters, cousins, mothers, aunts and grandmothers – and the number of adult females in each pride remains remarkably constant, regulated by the females themselves. Though the majority of young females are able to stay on in the pride of their birth, there are times when this is too much of a strain on the pride's resources, and they are forced to leave.

Holding a territory is everything to lions, and the size of a territory varies according to the availability of prey and the density of lions in the surrounding area. Schaller found that most lion prides in the Serengeti lived in the woodlands, where buffaloes, warthogs and topis are resident year round. But he also spent time observing lions on the treeless Serengeti plains and realized that they had had to adopt a very different way of life.

For as long as the migration of wildebeest and zebras blackens the plains the killing is easy for any lion. But as the dry easterly winds begin to pick up in late May and early June the wildebeest and zebras move out, with some of the animals heading directly north to the Mara, where – thanks to the higher rainfall – they can find plenty of grass and water to sustain them during the dry season. Species that can survive on the waterless plains, such as ostriches and Grant's gazelles, are hard for lions to catch. Consequently many of the lions attempting to eke out an existence on the plains are nomads – exiles from the pride system who are trying to avoid confrontation with members of the woodland prides, and if possible establish a pride of their own. Some of them follow the herds of wildebeest and zebras north, and if they are lucky manage to acquire a territory somewhere along the way. Those who choose to remain face hard times, digging warthogs from their burrows in the rock-hard earth, robbing cheetahs and wild dogs of their kills, and warring with the hyena clans.

Once in a while the Serengeti plains receive enough rainfall to provide sufficient grass to nourish topis, hartebeest and warthogs year round, and when this happens the nomads are quick to try to establish territories there. But it's always a precarious existence, and a tough way for lions to raise young. If a lioness is to be a successful mother she needs to be part of a pride, with access to a reliable supply of food and full-time male protectors to keep at bay the nomads who might attempt to kill her cubs.

If you were to fly low over the migration of wildebeest and zebras as the herds spill into the Masai Mara you would see below you perfect lion country: rolling plains and acacia thickets divided up by intermittent watercourses (known as luggas) and patches of woodland. These natural geographical features influence the distribution of prey, which in turn determines the number of lions each area can support. Prides have carved up every part of the Mara into a patchwork of territories; there is nowhere where you don't find lions. Some of the pride territories are as small as 30km² (12sq. miles) – others are four times the size. Lions are fairly flexible in their ability to adapt to different kinds of habitats, from prey-rich environments such as the Mara to the harshness of life in the Kalahari Desert in Botswana, where lions roam huge areas in the dry season to try and find sufficient food; one pride in Etosha National Park in Namibia is known to have had a home range of 2075km² (830sq. miles). With so much resident prey and the annual influx of hundreds of thousands of wildebeest and zebras, the Mara has everything a lion could need.

The boundaries of a pride's territory are flexible and seasonal, and may shrink or contract over time. Natural landmarks such as rivers, valleys or hillsides define some territories, though the Mara River is no barrier to a lion or a leopard, despite their dislike of getting wet, and the Marsh Pride sometimes crosses en masse to 'moonlight' in the territory of the Kichwa Tembo Pride

Nomadic male lions on the Serengeti short-grass plains. During the rains the southern plains turn green with new shoots, attracting wandering herds and the predators that feed on them.

Pride males play a vital part in lion society. By patrolling, scent-marking and roaring, they define the extent of their territory, discouraging other males from encroaching.

in the Mara Triangle – and vice versa. For the most part, the boundaries are invisible to the human eye, marked by scent sprayed onto bushes by the males, the physical presence of the lions themselves and their far-carrying roars. Each pride member has a well-defined sense of home. Home is the place where a lioness can find shade in the heat of the day, somewhere that provides suitable ambush sites for capturing prey and a safe hiding place to rear young cubs. This is the core area – the heart of the territory – that a pride defends most

tenaciously. As lionesses do the majority of the killing, protecting their hunting grounds is of primary importance and they are quite prepared to fight with other females to enforce their claim to the area. But they still need pride males to keep rival males from encroaching on their territory and killing their cubs.

The pride's 'home' has a different significance for males, for whom a territory is primarily about breeding rights. In prey-rich habitats such as the Mara they can generally rely on getting sufficient food

from kills made by the females, and from scavenging from hyenas: they have little need to hunt for themselves. Their biggest concern is keeping potential competitors from penetrating the territory and taking control of their females. Sex is a powerful influence in life and male lions will attempt to mate with oestrus females from other prides if they find them unguarded. Similarly a lioness in oestrus will sometimes accept a strange male, but first he has somehow to slip past the protective presence of her pride males, and in

Pride members sometimes gang up against an individual and harass them – albeit briefly – as these Topi Plains lionesses are doing to a young female relative.

relatively open country such as the Mara, that is not easy to do. With so much at stake it is hardly surprising that males and females are particularly hostile to non-pride members of their own sex.

A territory is passed on from one generation of lionesses to the next, an enduring matriarchy. Pride males come and go over the years – they do not build dynasties, but are forced on their way or killed by a new generation of lion kings. All young males leave their natal pride when they are two to four years old – either voluntarily or due to the increasing aggression of the adults of both sexes. This helps to prevent inbreeding. Brothers, half-brothers and cousins of a similar age leave together – the more the better – and become nomads. In lion society it is

generally the larger coalitions that sire the most cubs and dominate the largest groups of females, sometimes controlling a number of prides. If a young male is unfortunate enough to have no male relatives to join him when the time comes to leave his pride, he will try to form an alliance with one or two other nomadic males; otherwise, his chances of taking over a pride and siring cubs are slim.

Male lions rarely manage to acquire a territory until they are four or five years old. By that time they are fully grown and usually have a well-developed mane, which in most cases continues to fill out and may darken as they get older. To breed successfully the young males must oust the resident pride males from a territory, often by force, though if a group of newcomers is

large enough it can virtually walk in and take over, such is the power of numbers. These nomadic males (and pride males trying to gain control of a second pride) are cub killers – it is their way of ensuring that the lionesses come into season and breed with them once they have established themselves in the area. By killing any young cubs they also help to ensure that there is less competition for food when their own offspring are born. It is a tough life, far removed from the popular view of male lions as lazy animals interested only in stealing their next meal from the lionesses or hyenas. After dark and out of sight of visitors, there's a territory to be patrolled and marked, fights to be won. And, as we will see, in some parts of Africa male lions kill a large percentage of their own food.

Males are under pressure to acquire a territory as soon as they are able, for the simple reason that they have far shorter reproductive lives than females. They are past their prime by the time they are nine or ten years old, and probably fewer than 10 per cent of males live more than 12 years in the wild; many live considerably less. Females live up to 15 years (the record for Serengeti is 17) and continue to produce cubs for most of their adult life. This is reflected to a degree in the way males and females defend their territories. For females this involves a lifetime of boundary disputes that don't necessarily have to be resolved immediately. Hence they adopt a more cautious approach to trespassers than males do, rarely mounting a serious attack on their neighbours unless they significantly outnumber them. But males have no time to waste; a challenge from a rival coalition can mean an end to breeding, possibly an end to life. Once

males have laid claim to a group of females they must do everything within their power to hold on to them.

Generally lions of both sexes stake out as much territory as they can hope to defend. Certain prides of females prosper year after year, and may even expand their territories, driving out less powerful and numerous rivals and providing more room to accommodate young females. Sometimes when a pride produces a large group of young lionesses, the youngsters may even form a separate pride in part of their natal territory or end up displacing their older female relatives. At other times a pride simply ceases to exist, reaching a genetic dead-end with too few females to hold on to the territory and insufficient surviving offspring to rebuild the pride. The males' role in all this is one of opportunism. Having won control of a pride they may try to expand their realm of influence to incorporate more than one

group of females (hence a male coalition's territory may be bigger than that of any one pride). But even when this happens the females maintain their pride's identity and hold fast to their own territory.

Apart from a brief attempt to discover how many lions there were in the Mara, for many years the scientific community ignored the king of beasts in this part of East Africa. It wasn't until Joseph Ogutu, a young Kenyan student from Moi University in Nairobi, completed his study of the Mara's lions in 1992 that we gained a clearer picture of the number of lions living in the reserve, and of their social structure.

During a 16-month period Ogutu crisscrossed the entire reserve in his search for lions. But lions can be frustratingly elusive: at times members of a pride may be scattered across the whole 100km² (40sq. miles) of their territory, or they may all congregate in one place, making it difficult for an observer to find them and estimate

Serengeti pride males. The larger coalitions of males tend to hold territories for longer and sire more cubs.

numbers. Lions with territories at the periphery of the park often keep hidden during the daytime to avoid unnecessary contact with the Masai, and none of the lions were or are radio-collared.

To encourage lions to reveal themselves, Ogutu adopted a tried-and-tested method which biologist Butch Smuts had used with great success in the course of his work in the Kruger in South Africa during the 1970s. Using portable loudspeakers, he broadcast recordings of hyenas at a kill: a mixture of raucous whoops, growls and cackles – sounds that few lions could resist investigating in the hope of scavenging a meal. As one might expect, it was often male lions who emerged first from their resting places. With so many visitors scouring every part of the Mara in their eagerness to see predators, drivers and guides were able to provide Ogutu with a baseline for the numbers of males and females in each pride, enabling him to supplement and verify his own estimates.

By the end of his study, Ogutu had located 22 prides and was able to identify most of the pride members – a total of 484 lions, averaging 22 lions per pride. Added to this were 74 nomads (78 per cent of whom were males), giving a total population of 558 lions. If cubs of less than one year old were excluded, the total number of lions was 457, giving a density of 0.30 per km$^2$ or roughly three lions per

10km$^2$ (4sq. miles). Only Lake Manyara in Tanzania, which is about half the size of the Mara, has a higher density of lions: both areas support good populations of prey year round, the key factor determining lion densities in protected areas.

The smallest pride in the Mara at this time was the Kichwa Tembo Pride, consisting of two males, four females and two young cubs – a pride in its infancy, having recently been the object of a takeover by new males. Sadly, it has all but vanished now, apparently killed by Masai herdsmen as a political statement to avenge the loss of title to their land. The only survivors of the attack were an elderly lioness and her young daughter.

As Ogutu's study showed, nomads make up a relatively small part of the lion population and roam singly or in pairs or small groups. During Schaller's time in the Serengeti, he estimated there were about 400 nomads among the Serengeti's 2,000 lions, a somewhat higher percentage than in the Mara. These comprised young males and females forced from their natal pride as subadults, as well as adult males who had been robbed of their pride by new males, and lions who had been born and raised as nomads. But though they might appear to be outcasts, nomads are an important reservoir of new blood. Lions who are surplus to requirements today are the potential territory holders of tomorrow. No

lion chooses to be a nomad – it is a life full of danger, of trying to keep out of trouble with the established order, of struggling to find enough food.

The largest pride in Ogutu's study was the Talek Pride living in the east of the reserve, with four males, 17 females and 27 subadults and cubs – a total of 48 lions. The Talek River has always been an area where big prides prospered, though you rarely if ever see all of the members of a large pride together. I met this pride one morning on my way to Keekorok Lodge. Never in my life had I seen so many lions together. I counted 35 of them sprawled in the shade of a yellow-barked acacia tree, while a single lioness lay guarding a buffalo kill at the edge of a thicket. I marvelled at their confidence, a picture of power in repose, without a care in the world, a striking portrait of the benefits of being part of a substantial group.

Ogutu found that almost half the Mara prides had ten or more lionesses, and the largest prides all had coalitions of either three or four males. Prides around the Musiara area where the Marsh Lions live tend to be somewhat smaller than this, with six to eight lionesses more the norm. In general the largest prides are concentrated in the south and east of the reserve, territories with good populations of resident prey. Prides in these areas seem to be exposed to the migration of wildebeest

*We met the old female on a recent safari to Governor's Camp after she had crossed the river into Marsh Lion territory. At first we thought it was a hyena lying at the edge of a clump of reeds, but when she lifted her head we realized it was a lioness. She was probably about 15 years old and reminded Angie and me of a member of the Kichwa Tembo Pride known as the Old One, whom we had been following when Ogutu began his study of the Mara lions. Though still retaining pride membership, old females such as these often find it increasingly difficult to hunt for themselves or to battle for their share of a kill, and they gradually lose condition. This female was a pathetic sight, her frail body dwarfed by her massive head. She was skin*

*and bones, with open wounds on her back and hindquarters, and she could barely walk. We wondered if she would suffer the same fate as the Old One, forced to steal livestock from the Masai bomas and pay for her transgressions with her life.*

*A week or so later we heard that the old female had been found dead out on the plains. Perhaps she simply lay down and died before the hyenas could finish her off. But the chances of her daughter enjoying a long life seem remote. Without the support of female relatives it won't be long before a new group of lionesses lays claim to the area and drives her away. The only certainty is that her life as a nomad will be a hard one.*

Having stolen a topi calf from the hyena who killed it, the Topi Plains Pride dispute possession of the carcass. The adult female was able to dominate her younger relatives and keep the meal for herself.

and zebras for longer than their rivals further to the north, an important bonus when it comes to raising cubs.

About half of the prides in the Mara had two pride males, 23 per cent had three pride males and 18 per cent had four. This is similar to Schaller's findings in the Serengeti, with two male being the commonest number. In Nairobi Park and Lake Manyara in Tanzania, small parks with a high density of lions, one or two pride males are sometimes sufficient to control two or more prides. In fact a single male called Scarface controlled the whole of Nairobi Park during Rudnai's three-year study, mating with lionesses from all four prides, having ousted the previous single territory holder. But in the Serengeti and Mara it is virtually impossible for a single male to hold sway with a pride for long. There are just too many groups of males competing for the chance to claim a territory or acquire another one, and to date a single lion has never succeeded in taking over a pride territory in Serengeti.

The takeover of a pride by new males can be a dramatic affair, marked by vicious fights between rivals. The arrival of the migration in the Mara from the Serengeti in June or July often spells trouble for pride males, with bands of young nomads following the path of the great herds as a way of ensuring sufficient food. Sometimes trouble festers for months, with a coalition (or coalitions) of nomadic males wandering through territories that are already occupied, watching and listening, biding their time as they assess the most vulnerable pride to try and take over. This may so unnerve the resident males that they flee without a fight when challenged – particularly if they are old or the newcomers outnumber them and are too powerful to confront. But when a pride male finds himself cornered on his own or the contestants are well matched a fight may ensue.

Such fights often take place at night. By morning the only signs of battle are tufts of coarse hair torn from manes, blood splashed across the ground or even a dead or seriously wounded lion, with the perpetrators lying off to one side. It is not uncommon to see pride males with cuts inflicted by razor-sharp claws or deep puncture wounds from powerful canines, though these may also be the result of spats with other pride members over possession of food or oestrus females.

The tenure of the more successful coalitions lasts for two to six years. These are the fortunate ones; others are ousted again within a few months of a takeover. When you look into the baleful eyes of an old male lion, his magnificent mane now somewhat tatty, his face scarred from countless battles, with broken-down canines and missing incisors, hobbling along on three good legs – you are looking at a true survivor. Three-quarters of male lions die violently: either killed by poachers and trophy hunters or vanquished in fights with other males. Man is right to revere the power of the lion; they are indeed warrior kings.

# The Marsh Lions

Facts and figures can do no more than provide the raw skeleton of an animal. To understand lions you have to live with them, follow their every move, day after day, year after year. Mitsuaki Iwago, one of the world's great wildlife photographers, who spent more than a year and a half photographing the lions of the Serengeti and Ngorongoro Crater, was right when he said, 'You have to become the lion.' Iwago had no background in zoology and was a photographer first and foremost – he just happened to take great pictures of wildlife. But by becoming one with the lion he opened a window into their world that was far more powerful than the dry words of science. A sense of living with the pride is what *Big Cat Diary* tries to capture, both as observer and from the lion's perspective.

The Marsh Lions are one of the best known prides in the Mara and one of the reasons for choosing this area as our film base. The *Big Cat Diary* camp is hidden from view among the shade of African greenhearts and ancient fig trees overlooking the Mara River, about half a kilometre (quarter of a mile) north of Governor's Camp. The river forms the western boundary of the Marsh Lions' territory, an area of about 50km² (20sq. miles), and once in a while lions wander into camp as if to remind us that this is their land too. Drivers from Governor's Camp follow the happenings of the Marsh Pride on a daily basis: lions are the one animal that visitors must see on safari. So we are always assured of plenty of help in tracking them down.

The Marsh Pride is named after Musiara Marsh, which stretches southwards for a kilometre (two-thirds of a mile) or more from the spring which gives it birth towards Governor's Camp: a band of lush green sedges and tall grass frequented year round by elephants, waterbucks and buffaloes. The lions generally use the marsh only during the dry season when the dense reed-beds attract wandering herds of wildebeest and zebras, which come to drink and feed

Grey crowned cranes at sunrise. There are more than 500 species of birds in the Mara, and Musiara Marsh is one of the best places to look for herons, storks, plovers, sandpipers and kingfishers, to name but a few.

here. For most of the rest of the year the Marsh Pride congregates along the Bila Shaka lugga to the east of the marsh. This is the heart of their territory, which is why the drivers sometimes refer to these lions as the Bila Shaka pride. It has always been a favourite place for the lionesses to hide their young cubs, and generations of Marsh Lions have been born among the patches of croton bushes that surround the lugga. Bila

Shaka means 'without doubt' in Swahili. That's how certain the drivers from Governor's Camp are that they can find lions here.

In all the years we have known the Marsh Lions the pride has averaged five or six adult lionesses – never fewer than four – and two pride males. Whenever young females have tried to stay on as adults – unless there is a vacancy due to

Scar of the Marsh Pride. A large mane makes a male more imposing and probably indicates good genes to a potential mate.

the death of one or more of the lionesses – either they or their older relatives have ended up being exiled from part or all of the territory. But one way or another the matriarchy has continued, year after year. Only once – when I first started watching the Marsh Lions in 1977 – have there been more than two males with this pride. On that occasion there were three: Brando, Scar and Mkubwa (the big one). A few years later a coalition of four young nomads initially took over the Musiara area, then quickly split into two groups of two males each. These males became the pride males for separate groups of females living at Bila Shaka and the Marsh respectively, at which time there really was a Marsh Pride and a Bila Shaka Pride – the original Marsh Pride had split in two. This seems to underline the fact that any given area can sustain only a certain number of lionesses, and that the larger coalitions of males either eventually split up or invest their energies in winning breeding rights with larger prides of females. The ability to kill sufficient prey to

feed three or more adult males may play a part in this as the smaller prides of females generally do not kill buffaloes – the only resident prey that is large enough to provide sufficient food for their cubs and a large coalition of males.

The Marsh Lions have provided Angie and me with wonderful game-viewing over

Scruffy, Scar's companion. Not all males develop fine manes, and Scruffy and Scar couldn't have looked more different.

the years, but they proved to be a bit of a disappointment during the first series of *Big Cat Diary*. That year the migration remained in the Marsh Lions' territory week after week, and with so many wildebeest moving back and forth across the Bila Shaka lugga the lions hardly had to move, simply lying in ambush at the edge of the lugga and killing mainly at night. On many occasions the lions made multiple kills and invariably when we drove out to find them each morning, we would find that they had already eaten and retreated to the croton thickets, rarely moving for the rest of the day. The film crew whose job it was to spend all day and every day with the Marsh Lions struggled to film a single kill and everybody got very frustrated by the lack of

action. To make matters worse the pride didn't have any young cubs for us to film until the series was almost over. Apart from being cute, cubs increase the amount of social activity in the pride and are always good to film. I was grateful that I had the leopards to follow as well as the lions, and could spend time with Half-Tail and her young daughter Shadow. I'd far rather watch a leopard doing nothing than a lion.

We would have had plenty of action if only the cameras had still been up and running a few months later. Chaos broke out in Marsh Lion territory as a coalition of two nomadic males tried to take over the pride. Though older than their rivals and past their prime, the Marsh males were determined to stand and defend their territory. The males were well matched and after a number of skirmishes, a vicious fight ensued and the Marsh males were forced to flee. But it didn't end there. One of the pride females had recently given birth to cubs and was badly injured trying to defend her offspring from the new males. Eventually a semblance of order settled over the pride, the two males mated with the Marsh females and a new generation of cubs was born, though none of them survived to maturity.

The two new pride males, known as Scruffy and Scar, were an odd couple. They looked very different and were almost certainly not related, probably nomads who had forged an alliance of mutual benefit: nearly half of such twosomes in the Serengeti are non-relatives. Joining forces gave Scar and Scruffy the muscle to win battles with other coalitions of males, and they featured prominently in the second series of *Big Cat Diary*, filmed in autumn 1998. That was the year of the infamous buffalo attack on the Marsh Pride, when a herd of buffaloes went on the rampage among the thickets of the Bila Shaka lugga, killing one of the young cubs. Buffaloes are quick to try and intimidate lions, harassing and mobbing them, forcing them to give way. This decreases the likelihood that the lions will attack them, and driving the predators away allows the buffaloes to get on with feeding undisturbed. Lions generally obey this convention during the daytime, unless there is a sick or injured buffalo or a calf that they can cut out from the herd – though even then the herd may well respond to the stricken animal's bellows of distress by running en masse to its defence. It is very difficult for lions to defend young cubs from a determined group of buffaloes. If they are lucky the cubs may be able to scramble into a bush or, better still, up a stout tree. Sometimes they are just too young to do so.

My overriding memory of that battle between the Marsh Lions and the buffaloes is of the noise – and the powerlessness of the lions to keep the buffaloes at bay. The frightened, angry growls and rumbles of the lionesses matched the bellicose snorts and grunts of the buffaloes. It was terrifying. The thump of the buffaloes' heavy bosses as they rammed their horns into the ground, attempting to crush the life from the terrified cubs, was bone-chilling in its power and aggression. Their technique is brutal in its simplicity: a pile-diving downward blow followed by a lighting flick of the horns, tossing their victim high in the air or simply trampling it underfoot. It was a miracle that only one cub was killed and testimony to the bravery

*I've witnessed many interactions between lions and buffaloes and have the greatest respect for the power and tenacity of both. Being attacked by a buffalo has to be the worst nightmare of anyone who lives in the bush – apart from being grabbed in the jaws of a crocodile, crushed by an angry cow elephant defending her calf or horned by a black rhino! The problem with a buffalo is that it's unlikely simply to knock you over, assume you're dead and canter on over the horizon. No, a buffalo is going to toss you into the air, pound you into the ground, horn you and tread all over you with its cleats. If you survive such an attack you are one of the lucky ones. People say it's better to flatten yourself on the ground if you can't find a tree to climb when chased by a buffalo. You won't outrun it, and lying down might save you from being tossed or knocked to the ground. But I wonder?*

Old bull buffaloes remain in bachelor groups year round. Subadult males and prime breeding males also form bachelor herds during the dry season when no breeding is taking place.

One of the Topi Plains lionesses greets the younger pride male and solicits his attention, typical behaviour for a female in oestrus.

of the lionesses as they tried to lure the buffaloes away from their cubs, sometimes coming within inches of being tossed on the shiny black tips of those heavy hooked horns. Many an adult lion has been killed or badly injured in an altercation with buffaloes, and the benefit of being part of a herd was there for all to see.

The biggest surprise that day was how differently Scruffy and Scar reacted to the threat to their cubs. Scar was a magnificent lion; heavy-bodied with a luxuriant ginger-brown mane and black chest hair, while Scruffy, though a big animal, had a scruffy mane that remained sparse throughout his life. When the buffaloes launched their attack, Scruffy charged into the fray, initially as keen as the lionesses to defend their cubs. Not Scar. He retreated to the safety of the thickets, prowling around the periphery, moving only when forced to by the rampant mob of buffaloes, who were

incensed by the sound and scent of the lions. It was the classic case of looks not being everything. I would love to give Scar the benefit of the doubt and put his behaviour down to his lumbering size. Scruffy was quicker on his feet, and so were the lionesses. Perhaps it was just too much of a risk for Scar to confront the buffaloes. Whatever the reason, he wasn't getting involved.

This incident underlined the fact that each lion is an individual with its own temperament and character – and not in an anthropomorphic way. The broad brushstrokes that paint a picture of how lions live still apply, while taking into account the impact that their environment can have in altering their behaviour. By good fortune or good genes some lions are bigger than their companions or rivals, some are quicker, braver, more ready to fight on or to flee, and some are better

hunters than others. There are lions that are testy and irritable, preferring to be left on their own rather than socializing very much with their pride mates. Some are nervous and reactive, others more placid and slow to become aggressive. It is not just a question of temperament, either. The fact that 'looks' can make a difference has certainly been proved to be the case with lions, even if Scar was a slouch on this occasion.

It has always been assumed that the possession of a big mane might confer advantages on male lions – besides the obvious protection it offers in reducing injuries to the head and upper body during fights. When scientists put this to the test in the Serengeti, they found that males with large, dark manes were more successful than other males. Males tend to 'stand tall' when they are trying to impress a rival or court an oestrus female, adopting a broadside position and wheeling somewhat crab-like around the target of their display. A large mane certainly makes a male look bigger and is more intimidating in these circumstances, whether viewed head on or from the side. A black mane tends to stand out even more, adding to the sense of power, making the owner more obvious from a distance and providing a clear signal to young rivals to make themselves scarce. The study showed that females tended to prefer to mate with big-maned males, presumably because a big mane is a sign of good health and good genes. A male's mane continues to grow and may darken as he gets older, so it is also a good indicator for a female of a successful male – one who has survived.

No other member of the cat family shows such marked sexual dimorphism – physical differences between males and females – though male cats are bigger than females across all species. The significance of a mane may be linked to the lions' move into open country, where such a strikingly visual display is at its most effective. Lions can spot another lion from kilometres away and being able easily to distinguish male from female gives individuals of both sexes more time to decide on their response: to stay put, fight, flee or mate.

When a lioness first comes into oestrus she is not yet ready to ovulate. For that to happen she has to mate. This is a characteristic shared by all members of the cat family, a process called induced ovulation. A male cat's penis is covered with spines pointing away from the tip, roughenings that may play a part in stimulating ovulation and are perhaps the reason why a lioness often reacts aggressively as the male dismounts, turning round to snarl and slap at him as if in pain. During mating the male sometimes reaches forward and spreads his jaws wide across the female's nape, reminiscent of the way a lioness reaches down to pick a small cub up in her jaws, causing it to remain still. Perhaps this gesture is intended to have a similar effect on the lioness, pacifying her and preventing her from moving around, though she still may turn and clout the male when he is finished. Induced ovulation seems to be an adaptation to a solitary way of life, so it could be thought of as a disadvantage for a social species such as lions.

Most adult cats tend to avoid each other and live in large home ranges, so it often takes time for a male territory holder to track down an oestrus female in his territory or for her to find him. A male does this by reading the hormone content in the female's spray markings and by responding to her call (leopard females call and scent-mark more frequently when they are in oestrus and actively search out a mate). The fact that the female doesn't ovulate until mating occurs certainly works well for solitary cats. It not only gives the territory holder time to find the female when she is in oestrus, but also allows him the chance of chasing off any other male who might have found her first. But lionesses don't mark their territory by spraying scent on rocks or bushes in the way both male and female leopards do (though you will sometimes see lions of both sexes scuffing the ground with their back feet while peeing, leaving a visible and presumably smelly mark on the ground and then trailing their scent round with them, on their paws). The closer association between lions and lionesses in a pride makes it easier for the males to keep track of the reproductive status of their females.

A lioness announces that she is coming into season by a characteristic restlessness as well as by her scent. The males are able to monitor the situation by sniffing the ground where a lioness has peed and then lifting their heads and grimacing, wrinkling their noses and upper lips to reveal their massive canines – almost as if they were snarling, but uttering no sound. This lip curl is called flehmen and is commonly seen in antelopes, buffaloes, zebras and giraffes – in fact it occurs in most mammals except

Scar performing flehmen. This is something males do when they are investigating an interesting scent, particularly the urine of an oestrus female.

The larger of the two Topi Plains males showing a keen interest in one of the pride females. A male courting a female in oestrus stays as close to her as possible, guarding her against the approach of any other male.

for marine mammals and humans. Animals that exhibit flehmen have two small holes in the roof of the mouth just behind the front teeth – you can sometimes see them when a lion yawns. These are the openings of an olfactory organ known as the organ of Jacobson or vomeronasal organ, which is rich in sensory cells whose function is to analyse pheromones or scent molecules. Aside from testing if a female is in oestrus, cats perform flehmen whenever they come across a novel scent.

Once a male lion senses that a female is ready to mate he tracks her down and stays as close to her as she will allow – literally within a metre (3ft) or so – guarding her from his male companions. Other males in the coalition generally respect ownership, though with members of a group tending to travel together a fight may break out when they first find the female. But because lionesses often come into season together, particularly when new males have killed cubs, there is less need to fight. Also, it is not uncommon for a lioness to mate with more than one male during her oestrus cycle. Coalition partners tend to stay within the vicinity of the mating couple while making sure not to get too

close and incite a fight. Mating can last for up to five or six days, with the pair copulating on average once every 20 minutes. The frequency of mating is such that the first male may lose interest by about day four, having already mated hundreds of times, providing another male with the opportunity to mate with the same female. This helps to avoid undue competition on the part of pride males, and with neither male (if there are only two) knowing who fathered any cubs that are born they will both invest considerable effort in protecting them, though as it turns out one male usually fathers the whole litter.

Promiscuous as this may appear on the part of the females, they do sometimes exercise choice about whom they mate with. Generally there isn't a dominance hierarchy among male coalition members, unless there is a major discrepancy in size or age. If there is, a female may choose to mate with the older, bigger male. In fact she may have no choice if the bigger male prevents the younger male from getting near her. If a lioness doesn't wish to mate with a male she can simply lie down or sit down, aggressively rebuffing him whenever

he approaches her. She may do this anyway, when she first starts to come into season, but is not yet ready to mate. Another strategy is to keep on the move until she finds the male she is looking for. Sometimes you will see a female walking or trotting along for kilometre after kilometre, pursued by a male with whom she is reluctant to mate, seeking out a particular pride male she prefers and soliciting his attention. This may provoke a fight, but because every lion is equipped with formidable weapons it is only worth the risk of serious injury if the rewards are great; there is little advantage in injuring a pride mate and ally when it may take 1,500 copulations for every successful pregnancy. On average one in five oestrus periods results in cubs being born, but if the female fails to become pregnant she comes back into season in about two or three weeks, so the ability to produce a new litter isn't as precarious as it might seem.

Though the larger coalitions of males produce the most surviving offspring, it seems that only a few of the males – sometimes only one – sire most of the cubs. Coalitions of four or more males are always composed of relatives, so even if some of the males sire fewer offspring they end up helping to protect cubs that are related to them. Only among coalitions involving pairs of males, such as Scruffy and Scar, are matings usually shared equally over time – sufficient incentive for non-relatives to co-operate in the arduous task of defending a territory.

Roaring is a potent way of communicating for lions, and so is scent. They learn to recognize the sound and scent of each member of their pride as well as the roars and scent of other lions. This is vital for a social species. A roar can carry for 5km (3 miles) or more, allowing them to communicate over long distances and providing plenty of time for the appropriate response. If you can recognize the sounds of pride mates from far off you can keep in contact and meet up with whom you want to – your mother, your sisters or the pride males. Similarly, you are in a better position to determine where non-pride mates are and avoid meeting them – or challenge them if you so wish. This is probably why trespassers tend to keep quiet. Males mainly patrol their territories at night, shattering the silence with a series of impressive roars, proclaiming their territorial rights. To test the importance and function of roaring, scientists in the Serengeti used tape-recorded roars of known lions and played them to males and females. When the roars of males from a neighbouring pride were played to a group of females, the females hurriedly moved away, leaving their pride males to investigate. Whether the pride was in the heart of its territory – the core area – or on the periphery helped determine the lions' response. If there was more than one pride male present and they were well within their territory, the males always investigated the playback of roars of their male neighbours.

Interestingly, it was impossible to distinguish the response of coalitions of male relatives from those made-up of non-relatives such as Scruffy and Scar. When it comes to defending their territory unrelated companions co-operate as fully as if they were brothers. And there was no attempt to cheat on the part of non-relatives. A male approached the source of his neighbours' roars even when his companion was absent and unable to monitor his response. The bond between male companions needs to be as solid as rock, whether they are related or not. This is constantly reaffirmed in the way in which pride males solicitously greet each other and often rest close together, preferring their own company to that of the females. Forming tightly bonded groups is as important to males as it is to females – and to the success of any pride when it comes to breeding. Though pride females are naturally nervous about being confronted by neighbouring males,

particularly if they have cubs, they responded to the roars of neighbouring females when they were in their core area by moving out in readiness to challenge them. Even so, some were consistent laggards, regularly bringing up the rear or reacting only when there was little risk to themselves. Others responded to a challenge only when really needed. Lions have the power to make choices, to socialize with whom they want to.

Most people's image of lions is coloured by photographs and paintings depicting the pride: a group of lionesses surrounded by a gaggle of young cubs and subadults, with two or three adult males sporting luxuriant manes, close at hand and dominating the picture. In fact adult males and females lead rather different lives much of the time, and are often not together – the males may be off patrolling the territory, the females hunting or suckling their cubs. Life in the pride is a fluid web of relationships, with certain individuals associating with each

When lions are mating, the male often reaches forward and bites over the female's neck, inducing the same state of passivity as when a mother carries a young cub by the scruff of the neck.

other more frequently due to the closeness of their relationship and the needs of their offspring. Certainly, lionesses with young cubs form a tight-knit group or crèche within the pride. The crèche creates its own identity: the mothers do everything together, sharing the responsibility of raising their young, setting out to hunt as a group and mounting a formidable defence against male intruders. But lionesses only 'help' in this way when they have cubs of their own: a mother will not even share babysitting responsibilities with her adult daughter unless she herself has another litter of cubs at the same time.

Quite often, especially in a big pride, there may be a number of lionesses with different generations of cubs – or no cubs at all – and these may form subgroups within the pride for varying lengths of time. Though these groupings are still part of the pride and continue to recognize each other as such, they may lead more or less separate lives with different priorities according to the stage of their cubs'

development. Lionesses without cubs often lie up away from any crèches within the pride and may be less tolerant of young cubs, forming their own subgroup with other lionesses in the pride who do not have cubs and hunting on their own, which is probably to their advantage – fewer mouths to compete with for food and less pestering by cubs. Nevertheless, groups and individuals still sometimes join other members of the pride to socialize or to feed on a large kill, before wandering off again.

A heavily pregnant lioness looks like a barrel. She not only appears as if she's eaten an enormous meal but has tell-tale thickenings under the skin above her teats. She also often seems restless and rather uncomfortable in the heat of the day. Late in her pregnancy she becomes more secretive and begins to isolate herself from the pride as she searches for a place to give birth. It is not uncommon for a lioness to choose the area where she was born for her den site – sometimes the exact spot – if she is still a member of her natal pride.

Lionesses from the Marsh Pride have always favoured the croton thickets surrounding the southern end of the Bila Shaka lugga, which provide the perfect combination of good hiding places and a broad view of the surrounding plains. But in recent years the impact of dry-season fires and the Mara's large elephant population has destroyed much of the cover that this area used to offer. Other favourite birthplaces are caves in rocky outcrops, such as those in Leopard Gorge and along Fig Tree Ridge where Shadow the leopard and her daughter Safi can sometimes be found, and which they quickly abandon when lions are in residence. And the tall reed-beds in the heart of marshy areas such as Musiara Marsh also provide a secure hide-out for a lioness with young to protect.

Despite their mother's bulging girth, newborn lion cubs are tiny, with small ears, thick woolly fur and their eyes tightly closed. They weigh little more than 1.5kg (3lb), less than 1 per cent of their mother's weight. Their eyes open within ten days and

The Marsh Pride keeping a look-out for prey near Musiara Marsh, with the Siria Escarpment in the background. The numerous termite mounds provide an elevated view when the grass is long.

their milk teeth erupt at about three weeks, by which time they can walk – though perhaps stagger would be a better word to describe their movements. They can manage a run of sorts by the time they are a month old. Most females give birth to two to four cubs, though up to nine have been recorded in captivity. With only four teats, four cubs are quite sufficient for any lioness, and she soon shows signs of being suckled – damp brown matted hair around her nipples. The short gestation period of around 110 days means that if a lioness gives birth when conditions are not ideal and she loses her cubs, she is able to mate and produce a new litter again quickly.

A lioness will often hunt independently from the rest of the pride while her cubs are small, staying close to where she has hidden them. She will react aggressively to any other predator that might approach the area – and as any professional hunter will tell you, a lioness with cubs is almost certain to charge a human on foot. The Masai, who regularly walk through lion country on the periphery of the reserve, are much more cautious around lionesses with cubs than around the big males.

The dangers to small cubs are many. Large mongooses, pythons, martial eagles, jackals, hyenas and leopards are just a few of the predators that will kill and eat lion cubs if they find them – and nomadic lions are as big a danger as any. The cubs' only defence is to keep quietly hidden and not move around when their mother is absent. If disturbed, cubs utter explosive spitting noises that might startle and perhaps deter a small predator, but not a determined one.

To prevent scent from building up, the lioness licks her cubs' ano-genital region, stimulating them to pee or defecate on cue and then cleaning up after them. She will move her cubs every so often to a new location – sometimes only metres away from the old den site. A longer journey may be necessary if the lioness is unduly disturbed, such as when Masai herdsmen are grazing in the area, visitors drive too

Khali carrying a ten-week-old-cub (almost too big for her to manage).

close or predators or buffaloes pose a threat. She transfers the cubs one by one, carrying them in her mouth. The rest of the litter wait their turn, far safer at this stage than trying to follow their mother on foot. If the female were to run into trouble, at least she would only have the cub she was carrying to worry about, rather than losing the whole litter. A lioness caught in the open with young cubs by hyenas, for instance, could well find it difficult to defend them. At first the cubs would try and shelter beneath her, but the intimidating whoops and cackles of a mob of hyenas could easily cause them to panic and scatter, allowing the hyenas to pick them off one by one.

This period of isolation helps a lioness and her cubs to form a strong bond before she introduces them to the rich social milieu of life in the pride. By spending time alone together mother and cubs imprint their smell and call on each other. This is important in ensuring that the cubs know exactly who their mother is when confronted by the initially confusing hustle

and bustle of being part of a mass of cubs and adults, particularly when food is at stake. A soft 'augh' call, repeated as necessary, encourages her cubs to stay close to her.

Normally cubs are introduced to the pride when they are six to eight weeks old, but sometimes a female brings them into the open earlier than this or other members of the pride locate the mother and her cubs and begin to interact. If a number of lionesses become pregnant around the same time, which sisters often do regardless of whether they have lost cubs, then they may all give birth in the same locality and may visit one another while still keeping their cubs separate. Occasionally a lioness carries very young cubs to where the other lionesses are congregating, though this is far from ideal, particularly if there are older cubs who may be too rough with their younger siblings. Lionesses can be very aggressive when they have small cubs, flattening their ears, snarling and grunting, baring their huge canines and lunging towards any lion or lioness (or car) that tries to approach too closely. Lions learn from an early age the precise meaning of messages encoded in a wide range and combination of facial gestures, body language and voice – the threat and counter-threat, aggression and submission, that are vital in maintaining order among animals so capable of seriously injuring one another.

Pride males pose special problems for lionesses with young cubs. To gain control of a pride of females, males actively hunt down cubs sired by the previous territory holders, as it takes a female two years to raise her cubs to independence, too long for the new males to wait. In this respect, every pride male has probably killed cubs at some point in his life as a rite of passage on the path to owning a territory, and more than a quarter of all cubs die in this way. Consequently, a lioness who has had cubs killed by new pride males has every reason to be cautious about allowing the same males to gain access to her young – their young – until she feels confident that their intentions are not life-threatening.

One tactic a lioness employs to good effect with small cubs when a male approaches – or if her cubs try to socialize with the male – is to get quickly to her feet and block his path or push herself up against him, forcing him to stop or move aside. This lets the male see that he must be careful around the new cubs. Males generally respect this convention and appear keen to avoid confrontation with the lionesses in these circumstances.

Small cubs exhibit a mixture of caution and inquisitiveness when introduced to their pride mates. They desperately want to socialize but aren't sure at first how they will be received. Their mother's presence is the main factor dictating the outcome of these early attempts at socialization, and her level of aggression gradually wanes as her cubs become more confident and are able to interact with the other members of the pride without risk of injury. Within a week or so the cubs are initiating play with

older cubs or making a nuisance of themselves by biting the adults' tails.

Young cubs are particularly intrigued by the pride males, pushing up under their chins in greeting and losing themselves among their thick manes. Some pride males are incredibly tolerant of their offspring's antics; others are less accommodating and deter further games by batting the cubs away with a huge forepaw, snarling to

expose their thumb-sized canines or biting down on them, though not hard enough to injure them. Nevertheless, when lionesses have young cubs it is noticeable how attentive the males appear to be, often making the crèche the focus of their daytime resting place. This is a sensible precaution, as cubs are at their most vulnerable to infanticide during the first nine months and benefit greatly from the

The Marsh Pride's 12-week-old cubs being investigated by a two-year-old female relative. Cubs are usually kept hidden for the first six to eight weeks before being introduced to other members of the pride.

pride males' protection during this period.

Watching a group of lionesses surrounded by a gaggle of young cubs all eager to suckle, it's difficult to determine who belongs to whom. Cubs at times wander from one lioness to another, seemingly at random, trying to muscle in on a free teat, searching for anyone prepared to provide them with milk – mother, aunt or grandmother – any lioness who is lactating will do. You might well ask what is going on. Domestic cats give birth to large litters of kittens, which quickly establish a teat order when suckling – claiming an individual teat for themselves and generally maintaining this order until they are weaned. This happens within days of birth; presumably each kitten leaves its scent on its 'own' teat, so that after some initial squabbling they can simply get on with feeding themselves. This is certainly more comfortable for the mother than constantly having her teats scratched and torn, and is the most efficient way for the kittens to share their mother's milk. Leopard cubs also adopt a teat order and it seems likely that this is the norm for all the solitary cat species. But not for lions. Lion cubs will try and suckle from any teat that is vacant, regardless of whether or not it belongs to their mother.

One of Khali's cubs, aged ten weeks, chewing on a croton bush along the Bila Shaka lugga. Cubs' milk incisors erupt at three weeks and their canines at four weeks.

The younger of the Ridge Pride males with two of the pride's cubs, aged four to five months. Lions often drink after feasting on a carcass.

Communal suckling isn't quite as haphazard as it might appear. Lionesses certainly do recognize their own cubs and are generally more tolerant of being suckled by them. If bigger cubs try to suckle from a lioness who is not their mother, they are liable to be firmly rebuffed. She may push them away with her paw or snarl and grunt with open mouth to deter them. If she is really fed up all she has to do is roll over or get to her feet, often with cubs hanging for dear life on to her teats. But sometimes it's just too much bother to keep a cub away regardless of whose it is; and if a female has few cubs of her own she can afford to be generous with her milk and let other cubs suckle from her. She is more likely to do this when members of the crèche are close relatives, and the best time for a cub to makes its move is when a lioness dozes off, particularly if she isn't its mother. A lioness needs her sleep.

Forming a crèche of similar-aged cubs is the most efficient way for lionesses to raise their young. Cubs born around the same time will be of a similar size when they start to eat meat at about six to eight weeks of age. If, as often happens, their mothers hunt together, it may help to reduce competition with lionesses who have older generations of cubs within the pride. Gaining a share of the food at a kill can be tough, and older cubs tend to dominate their younger relatives. Some 25 per cent of cubs die simply because they are unable to get sufficient to eat.

The advantages of being part of a large crèche extend well beyond childhood. Young males will have a greater chance of success when the time comes to break away from their natal pride if they have plenty of brothers and male cousins of a similar age to leave with them. This initially makes the job of staying alive somewhat easier, allowing them a greater chance of killing large prey such as buffaloes and dominating hyenas at a kill. And as they mature into powerful adults, the larger the coalition, the easier it will be for them to take over a pride and raise lots of cubs. The same applies to any young females who are forced to leave their natal pride. The more companions they have, the greater the likelihood that they will be able to carve out a territory of their own and defend it from other females. Winning or inheriting a territory is everything to lions, regardless of their sex.

Khali's eight-to-ten-week-old cubs suckling among the safety of a thicket along the Bila Shaka lugga. Cubs are weaned by the time they are about six months old.

# Pride Takeover

The repercussions of a pride takeover can be devastating for the lionesses and their cubs. The social fabric of the pride is torn apart, and it may take up to two years for a semblance of order to return. Sometimes it never does, causing a split in the pride that refuses to heal, particularly when there is more than one generation of cubs, with mothers trying to protect litters of different ages. Lionesses have to use all their knowledge of the pride territory to ensure their cubs' safety. Their best form of defence is to keep on the move, and it helps if there are a number of females travelling together – more eyes and ears to detect danger and divert an attack. If a strange male approaches, regardless of whether or not they have cubs with them, the lionesses are likely to take the initiative, charging and snarling at the intruder, putting him on the defensive and doing everything in their power to force him to move away. But males are often not easily deterred, especially if they pick up the scent

A lioness in the Serengeti threatens one of three males, forcing him to back off. He is standing tall and adopting the typical sideways crab-like stance of a lion trying to intimidate a rival.

of cubs and recognize by the hostile reaction of the females that they have something to hide. Though lionesses are much smaller and less powerful than adult males they are quick and agile. Collectively they are a force to be reckoned with and may manage to hold a male at bay long enough for their cubs to escape and hide.

The older of the Topi Plains males courting a female and trying to prevent other members of the pride from approaching her. She threatens him with open mouth to deter him from harming her cubs.

Subadults of both sexes are a drain on the resources of the pride territory and competition for any cubs the new males might manage to sire. So it is to the new males' advantage to drive them away. Since their only interest is in gaining access to females who can breed with them, it is vital that they continue to pursue the adult females until they are ready to mate. Having killed off any small cubs and driven out the older ones, the males are now in a position to court the adult lionesses remaining in the territory.

Over the years the Marsh Lions have endured their share of pride takeovers and social disruptions. Yet the extent of their territory has remained remarkably constant, maintained through the continuity of generations of female relatives, adopting the same pattern of land tenure year after year. But they have other concerns besides competition with lions. The Marsh Lions'

territory overlaps the reserve boundary, forcing them to adapt to the challenge of living among the Masai and their livestock. There are no fences to keep the animals in or people out. In the old days the Masai followed a nomadic existence, patterned by the rains, moving with their cattle to wherever the grass was short and green. Their *enkangs* or homesteads were built from wattle plastered with cow dung, there was no permanence to their lives, no possessions to anchor them to one place. When they wanted to move they simply built another *enkang* and abandoned the old one to the soil. But in recent times the winds of change have begun to transform Masailand. The old ways are dying out; tin roofs and conical thatched houses are now a common sight. More people and more livestock crowd on to less land, and there is a growing permanency to their way of life that is incompatible with wild animals.

The Masai have never accepted that they should not be able to bring their cattle into the reserve, particularly in dry years when it is a struggle to find sufficient food for their livestock. The very idea of boundaries and land ownership is an alien concept. Traditionally cattle were owned, not land. Land is for everybody. The fact that the Masai are expected to share the land outside the reserve boundary with the wild animals, and to live in harmony with them, seems the greatest irony. During the dry season hundreds of thousands of wildebeest and zebras invade these pastures and the migration strips the land bare within weeks. The Masai feel that it is only fair that the government should reciprocate, and allow them to enter the reserve when times are hard and good grazing and water for their cattle are in short supply. The game rangers who police the reserve are all Masai from the surrounding communities;

Masai herdsmen and their cattle near the spring feeding Musiara Marsh.
Though the Masai are beginning to adopt a more sedentary lifestyle,
cattle are still the mainstay of their existence.

*During the filming of the third series of Big Cat Diary we could only watch as the Marsh Pride began to break apart. In fact Angie and I witnessed the beginning of the process six months before filming started in September 2000. The Marsh Lions were in trouble, their territory under siege on two fronts, forced to try and hold their own against incursions by the Masai herdsmen and battle with the pride males from the neighbouring Topi Plains Pride. For the past two years Kenya had suffered the ravages of one of the worst droughts in living memory. The dawn of a new millennium heralded the beginning of the third year in which the rains failed. Ironically, while most of life wilts and dies in the face of drought, predators generally prosper. Disease often follows the cycle of drought and starvation, and for the lions at least life is easy. Most predators – with the exception of the timid cheetah – are willing scavengers, and with so many animals dying around them there is often little need for the predators to kill for themselves. Buffaloes and hippos, two of the most water-dependent herbivores, were among the first to succumb.*

*In the drought of 1993 the Mara lost 80 per cent of its buffaloes, with the population declining from nearly 12,000 to 2,000 animals. As the drought intensified, the buffaloes were forced to split into smaller and smaller groups to find sufficient food and water. With this, the life-saving advantages of being part of a large herd were lost and the Marsh Lions took full advantage of the situation. Buffaloes need to drink every day, and*

Masai herdsmen bringing their cattle to water near Lake Magadi in the Great Rift Valley during the dry season. There are about 350,000 Masai in Kenya and Tanzania.

*all the lions had to do was to lie in wait for them near the last pools of water among the croton thickets bordering the Bila Shaka lugga. Sometimes the buffaloes were too weak to fight and their companions reluctant to counterattack for fear of becoming victims themselves; sometimes they were eaten alive. There was so much food that the lions could afford to eat the soft flesh around the animal's face and then abandon the carcass, particularly when wildebeest swept through their territory. Wildebeest have much softer skin and are easier to open up compared to gnawing through the leathery hide of a buffalo.*

*The Marsh Lions' cubs were barely a year old at the time of the '93 drought, and would normally have avoided such fierce adversaries as buffaloes. Instead they were able to practise their hunting skills, leaping onto the back of a buffalo or attempting to apply a killing bite over nose and mouth. These youngsters never forgot the experience they gained during this period and as adults proved adept at tackling even strong and healthy buffaloes. They had conquered their fears and replaced them with expertise, and for a while a 'culture' of buffalo killing became part of the Marsh Lions' identity.*

The Marsh Pride attacking a buffalo. Buffaloes are one of the first animals to succumb to drought, with herds splitting into smaller groups to try to find sufficient food, making them a target for prides of lions

Masai celebrating the final days of the *eunoto* ceremony, marking the transition between warriorhood and junior elder, after which the young men may marry and own cattle.

understandably sympathetic to the plight of their brothers, they find it hard to justify enforcing the rules. Little wonder then that the Masai herdboys sometimes drive their cattle into the reserve, ignoring the concrete pillars that announce the boundary separating the land of the Masai from the land of the animals.

Today, a permanent Masai village perches on a rise overlooking the length of the Bila Shaka lugga. During the wet season, when the area surrounding the lugga becomes waterlogged, the Marsh Lions are forced to leave the reserve and follow their prey to higher ground. Generally they manage to avoid conflict with the Masai by hiding in thick cover during the daytime. But with the onset of the dry season the Masai start to bring their cattle to drink at the spring that feeds Musiara Marsh, which lies just outside the reserve. This can pose a problem for the lions, who covet the marsh during the dry season, lounging in the muddy coolness of the dense reed-beds to ambush the wildebeest and zebras that daily come to drink here. Mostly the big cats remain

hidden until the Masai and their cattle have departed, tracking their movements by the tinkle of the cowbells and the flute-like whistling of the herdboys. But over the years there have been a number of incidents in which lions have taken livestock and been killed in revenge. Though these events have at times weakened the integrity of the pride, they have never threatened to destroy it. Until now.

As the drought worsened in 2002, more and more Masai from outlying areas moved into the Mara. Camped along the river, we could hear the sounds of cowbells as they brought their cattle into the reserve at night to avoid harassment by the authorities. Sometimes a vehicle would arrive from headquarters and round up the herdsmen; then the cattle would disappear. But never for long. During the middle of the day when most of the visitors were back at camp taking a siesta, we often found herds of cattle grazing along the Bila Shaka lugga, deep in Marsh Lion territory. When we approached the young herdsmen, they disappeared into the long grass. Some of the smaller ones even hid down warthog burrows or raced away and left us marvelling at their fitness. For the Masai it is a simple choice – cattle mean everything: they are the way a man measures his wealth, the bride price he must pay when he takes another wife; they are their most cherished possession, and even a half-starved cow is still of value. The local Masai chiefs told us that many of the herds came from outside the area. Despite the dire conditions that they themselves were suffering, they felt obliged to share their land with their brothers while times were so tough. It was hard to argue with that. But these particular lions – the Marsh Lions – had assumed a cult-like status to visitors to the northern Mara, and to us they were like old friends.

It was around this time that we heard that Scruffy, the Marsh male, had been killed. He had begun to roam further to the north and was said to have been courting a

lioness from a small group known as the Gorge Pride, which includes Leopard Gorge in its territory. But when Scruffy and the lioness killed a cow, the Masai tracked them down to a dense croton thicket and speared them to death. No herdsman or rancher is going to tolerate a stock-raiding lion, particularly if nobody is going to compensate him for his loss. To add to the Marsh Pride's woes, over the next few months two of the lionesses disappeared, almost certainly as a result of conflict with the Masai, reducing the pride to just three adult females.

Scruffy's wanderlust would cost his pride dearly. It had the same effect as if new males had entered the Marsh Pride's territory and killed one of the pride males. But it wasn't a group of young nomads that now posed a threat to the Marsh Lions. To the east of Bila Shaka lies the land of the Topi Plains Pride, numbering more than 20 lions, including two big, blond-maned males. The pride is often to be found crowded around a kill out on the plains or crammed into the shade of one of the gardenia bushes in an area known in the Masai language as Naiboisoit – the place of white stones. It is a beautiful area in the lee of Rhino Ridge, affording stunning views of the surrounding Topi Plains, where you are always assured of finding large numbers of topi, an antelope somewhat smaller than a wildebeest with distinctive plum-coloured thighs. Spotted hyenas den here year round and regularly prey on the topi that breed on the plains each year.

In February and March the topi males rut, dropping to their knees and jousting with their horns, testing each other and establishing dominance. Each successful male marks out a small territory, and when a female comes into oestrus she moves onto the breeding ground or lek, as these tightly packed territories are known, and selects a mate. We have often watched as a hyena rouses itself from a mud wallow in the middle of the day and ambles nonchalantly around the lekking ground, checking for males who have lain down to rest, exhausted by the arduous task of defending their territory, displaying and mating. If the topi fails to stir the hyena rushes in, grabbing its victim high up on the shoulder or by the flank and pulling it over. Before the startled animal can struggle to its feet, the hyena tears at the topi's soft belly skin and is often joined within seconds by other hyenas. Sometimes members of the Topi Plains Pride are attracted by the frantic sounds of feeding and come rushing over to steal the kill.

Emboldened by the loss of Scruffy, the Topi Plains males now began to venture down to the Bila Shaka lugga, spending more and more time away from their females. It is not at all uncommon for pride males to do this, seeking out mating opportunities with lionesses in adjacent prides, if they can dominate or drive out the resident males. This is something that the larger coalitions – numbering three or four males – are more easily able to do, and one reason why they sire so many cubs. But with only a single male now defending the Marsh Pride territory, it was an opportunity that the two Topi Plains males couldn't resist. They had already sired more than a dozen cubs with the six lionesses in the Topi Plains Pride, most of whom were about a year old, big enough to accompany their mothers wherever they wandered. So there was little risk of them being killed by other males, if their own fathers moonlighted.

We met the Topi Plains males one morning as they walked boldly down towards the Bila Shaka lugga, sensing by their demeanour that they were looking for trouble. We could see some of the Marsh Pride lying flanked around a massive termite mound at the edge of a dense patch of croton bush, one of their favourite resting-up places. The minute the younger of the Topi Plains males spotted the Marsh Lions he turned and trotted back up the rise. The older male paused, his blond mane billowing in the cool morning breeze. He seemed unconcerned that his companion was so quick to desert him and continued down to the lugga. We waited to see what would happen. On he came, nose to the ground, following the scent trail left by the Marsh Pride as they retreated to the safety of the lugga earlier that morning after feeding on a kill close to the Topi Plains Pride's territory. He moved more cautiously now as he entered the thickets lining the edge of the lugga. He already

The Topi Plains males making their way down to the Bila Shaka lugga to stir up trouble.

*The blond males were in peak condition. Both were fully grown, though one was older and bigger-bodied than his companion. If they were related they were probably born to different mothers in the same pride; or, like Scruffy and Scar, they might be former nomads who had joined forces in order to win a territory. The Topi Plains males not only looked different, they acted differently. The older, larger male was always first to initiate a foray into Marsh Lion territory, displaying the confidence of a lion who had done this kind of thing before. He was the one who wanted to push on whenever he saw that some of the Marsh Lions were in residence, while the younger male was quick to turn back, long before danger threatened. This difference in temperament may have been due simply to the fact that the younger male was smaller and less experienced than his companion. But as we had already seen with Scruffy and Scar, being the biggest lion doesn't necessarily mean that you will be more willing to take risks or be tougher and more aggressive. It was fascinating to watch how the younger of the two males eventually grew to equal his companion in size, and with the advantage of youth began to hold his own and even dominate him if it came to a fight over an oestrus female. But that wouldn't happen for another year yet.*

The Topi Plains males after one of a number of attempts to force Scar from his territory. Males are at their most co-operative when challenging other males and defending a territory.

knew from the scent trail that Scar wasn't with the pride.

By now the younger members of the Marsh Pride – the cubs born in 1998 – were sitting up, alert. These were the same cubs who had survived the attack by the herd of buffaloes and had endured the rigours of the long rainy season when food was often in short supply. There were eleven of them in all, ranging in age from one to one-and-a-half years, big enough to run for their lives if need be. They would not want to get involved in a scrap with a big male lion – certainly not a male from another pride, and certainly not if they themselves were young males, which four of the youngsters were.

The lionesses sensed something was wrong. Maybe it was the alertness of the younger lions, the scent of fear perhaps or a barely audible murmur. A ripple of tension now ran through the whole pride, bringing them to their feet. Bump Nose – the mother of the three youngest cubs –

ran head low towards the male, mouth open, hissing and grunting. He stopped, drawing himself up to his full height, standing tall to try and intimidate her, and for a moment seemed as if he was going to hold his ground and fight. But by now he could see a second lioness hurtling towards him, and at that he turned and bounded away through the croton, pursued by the two females. Some of the younger lionesses in the pride followed the adults' lead, while the four young males wisely stood and watched from a safe distance. Satisfied, the lionesses stopped and stared after the blond male, who trotted back up the rise to join his younger companion.

From that day onwards, Bump Nose abandoned the Bila Shaka lugga and moved with her cubs to the marsh. The eight older cubs soon followed. This was as far west as the Marsh Pride could move without crossing the river, and to do that would have risked confrontation with the Kichwa Tembo Pride. Here at least, among the

dense reed-beds and long grass, they were able to seek sanctuary and distance themselves from the Topi Plains males. Bump Nose became the focal point and leader for this group of young Marsh Lions, and they were quick to respond to her movements: wherever she went, they followed. The young lions still depended on the pride for food and protection, and right now the only pride they had was Bump Nose. Even at two years of age, lions are rather clumsy in their hunting efforts and vulnerable to attack by strangers, though less likely to be killed. So it was a somewhat cowed and nervous subgroup of the Marsh Pride that visitors met each morning when they started out on their game drives.

Over the next few weeks, the Topi Plains males made repeated forays into the Marsh Lions' territory, tracking the movement of these other lions by their roars and scent. Sometimes they found Scar still clinging to his domain. Big as he was, Scar was careful to keep his distance whenever the two males appeared. Alone he could not afford to stand and fight. Instead he would hurry on his way, occasionally turning to stand tall from a suitably safe distance, displaying his magnificent ginger mane and black chest hair, roaring his defiance. The sight of the solitary pride male served simply to provoke the two intruders to greater efforts, and they would come trotting towards him, their golden eyes set hard, mouths taut with aggression. The continued presence of the old male was like a nagging wound. They would not rest until they had banished him from the area.

The Topi Plains males now began to focus their attention on the other two adult Marsh lionesses. One of these we had named Khali – the angry one – because though good-natured, she was always the first to react if there was trouble. Khali had mated with both Scar and Scruffy shortly before Scruffy had been killed, and had since given birth to five cubs. Not surprisingly she had chosen the croton thickets of the Bila Shaka lugga, where she herself had been born, as their birthplace. Under other circumstances this would have been the sensible thing to do – it was after

all the favourite resting-up place for the whole pride when they were in the area, and provided security in numbers if strange males suddenly appeared. But the Marsh Pride had been seriously compromised by the loss of Scruffy and the other two lionesses. A pride of just three females will always struggle to hold a good territory in a place like the Mara, where there are so many lions. But for now they weren't even three – Bump Nose had her own role to play as matriarch to the group of eleven young Marsh Lions. For Khali things couldn't have been worse; there were no

Scar with Khali's cubs. Males generally interact with lionesses and cubs only at a kill or when a female is in oestrus.

other females with young cubs to form a crèche and help to defend the cubs against the Topi Plains males, and the other lioness in the pride was making herself scarce.

Despite the regular incursions by the Topi Plains males, Scar was determined to hang on to his territory for as long as he could. He had already proved on a number of occasions that he wasn't the bravest of lions. Such flaws in temperament might appear to lack survival value, but if you have companions to cover for you then perhaps not. He had already managed to sire cubs of his own that would soon be old enough to become independent, so by that measure he had led a successful life. As for the eleven young Marsh Lions, they were still very inexperienced, but were benefiting from being part of a large crèche. Nevertheless, with only one adult lioness accompanying them, they struggled at times to keep the hyenas at bay when a kill had been made.

Whenever Scar needed food he would head for the Marsh and parasitize the kills made by Bump Nose and the younger members of the pride. But most of the time he would actively seek out Khali and her cubs (or she would find him) among the croton thickets of the Bila Shaka lugga. The old male seemed to enjoy being with a fellow pride member and he was very tolerant of the little cubs when they forced their attentions on him. It seems unlikely that a lion 'knows' which are his cubs within the pride, but there was a good chance that Khali's cubs were Scar's, so his behaviour may have been an attempt to provide some measure of protection for his offspring. Khali seemed keen to solicit the attention of the lone male, though there was always the possibility that it might increase the chances of the Topi Plains males finding her and her cubs in their quest to locate Scar and drive him away.

Male lions adopt different strategies in trying to protect their offspring, depending on how wooded the habitat is and the kind of prey available to them. In the more open plains environment of the Mara and Serengeti, males spend more time with the pride, particularly when there are young cubs. This would appear to be the best way for them to protect their offspring when they are most vulnerable. Out on the plains it is easier for pride members to detect the movement of other lions. If strange males intrude and try to track down any cubs, the pride males may see them coming from afar and move out to intercept them; even if they don't see them immediately, they are close at hand to defend the cubs should the need arise. Over the years we have witnessed the Marsh lionesses succeed on a number of occasions in forcing nomadic males to leave the area before they could harm their cubs when the pride males were elsewhere. But the persistence of males in trying to kill cubs, and their massive strength, mean that many times the females fail to save their offspring from an untimely death. It would therefore make sense for the pride males to focus their efforts on staying close to the females within the core area of their territory when there are young cubs to protect. But there are other ways to achieve the same result.

Researchers in southern Africa have found that male lions living in wooded areas spend less time in the company of females and cubs than males living in more open habitats. In savanna woodland in Kruger, males invest more time in patrolling the boundaries of their territory (which are similar in size to those in the Mara and Serengeti), and in scent-marking and roaring as the most effective way of discouraging rivals from entering their territory, rather than staying close to their offspring. By roaming more widely males may also stand a greater chance of taking over another pride of females and siring additional cubs. But for males to be able to wander further afield, they have to be able to secure sufficient food, either by hunting for themselves or by scavenging.

In Kruger it is certainly not true that lionesses always do the hunting and that

males simple feast on the proceeds of their pride mates' efforts. Though males are ill-equipped to hunt the more fleet-footed species such as wildebeest and zebras that females target, those in savanna woodlands harbouring large buffalo populations gain most of their food from hunting for themselves. Killing a buffalo requires strength and co-operation rather than stalking prowess: coalitions of pride males and particularly groups of nomadic males frequently hunted and killed buffaloes.

**The Topi Plains Pride. Cubs practise their hunting skills by playing, stalking, chasing, pouncing and biting.**

They also hunted impalas, another species found in high densities in savanna woodlands. I have even witnessed this in quite open habitat in the Mara when a large male surprised a less than vigilant impala after a short rush and pounce. Where male lions rely less on the females to provide them with food, it also indirectly benefits their cubs, as there is less competition at a kill (though the fact that males sometimes let cubs feed and keep the females away would militate against this).

In the Mara and Serengeti, though pride males do sometimes kill for themselves – usually buffaloes – they rarely need to; the availability of prey is such that the females are able to provide sufficient food for the whole pride (though nomadic males often hunt for themselves here too), allowing them to stay together more often. The high density of hyenas in these savanna areas may also play a part in this. In more open habitats it is easier for all of the predators to know when a kill has been made and to find it. The presence of pride males at kills helps to deter the more numerous hyenas from stealing from the it, and thereby ensures more food for their cubs. As most lions in Africa live in savanna woodlands with high densities of buffaloes and impalas, rather than open plains environments, it seems likely that male lions hunt more often than was once thought. This illustrates yet again the considerable flexibility that exists in the way lions behave, prompted by their need to adapt to different environments and different prey.

This flexibility is mirrored by the behaviour of Asiatic lions, which look very similar to African lions except that they are smaller, with a distinct fold of skin running along the underbelly (this is only occasionally seen in African lions, more so in males) and the males have less pronounced manes – perhaps because there is less need to be conspicuous from a distance in thicker cover. Asiatic lions tend to form smaller groups than their African counterparts, probably because they hunt smaller prey such as the chital deer which weighs about 50kg (110lb). Male coalitions defend a territory of 100–140km$^2$ (40–55sq. miles), which may include more than one pride of females (female territories are about half the size). In the dense cover of India's Gir Forest males are able to stalk up on prey and hunt for themselves; they are also the main culprits in attacks on livestock that are an easy target for any lion. Because of this the males can spend much of their time on their own, patrolling their territory and seeking additional mating opportunities. They generally associate with the females only when the latter are in oestrus or have made a large kill – not because they have small cubs.

But whatever your strategy for defending your territory and your breeding opportunities, it can only work if there is a strong coalition to carry it through. For Scar, the options were now limited. Without a partner to help him kill buffaloes, he might even struggle to find sufficient food. It was unlikely at this stage

in his life that he could forge an alliance with a nomad to support him in his quest to hold on to the Marsh Lions' territory, thought this does sometimes happen. But by clinging on here Scar could at least scavenge enough from his pride mates to keep himself alive.

The other members of the Marsh Pride occasionally returned to the Bila Shaka lugga and joined Khali and her cubs – or vice versa. When they did it was as if they had never been apart. The sense of pride membership was still intact. By now Khali's offspring were quite accustomed to all the attention they received from the larger cubs, two of whom were their older brother and sister. These siblings were one and a half years old when Khali became pregnant with her latest litter, and it was interesting to see how differently she responded to her older offspring now that she had new cubs to provide for. It underlined the importance of the pride system, which continued to nurture these half-grown lions even when their mother was preoccupied with a new generation. They could still get food from the kills made by any pride member – if it was large enough. Even though Khali's half-grown daughter often sought the company of her age-mates at the marsh in trying to avoid conflict with the Topi Plains males, she would stay close to her mother when they met, greeting and being greeted, and she paid a lot of attention to her younger brothers and sisters. But whenever Khali's adolescent son approached the cubs, his mother would react aggressively towards him, threatening him with open mouth, snarling and forcing him to back off. This distrust of males on the part of lionesses with young cubs, even when those males are their own sons, was very apparent. Interestingly, Khali was a lot less aggressive toward the younger male cubs in the group who were just over a year old, one of whom became a great favourite with the tiny cubs and spent many hours in their company.

Everyone loves to watch and photograph a lioness with tiny cubs, and Angie and I

are no exception. The Marsh Lions are so used to vehicles that they simply act as if they weren't there. Sometimes we would find Khali moving her cubs one by one, carrying them in her mouth, staying close to the lugga. Even when the cubs were quite capable of walking and running beside her, she would sometimes stop and pick one of them up, striding along with it in her mouth as the rest of the litter grizzled at the pace she set. But by the time the cubs were eight weeks old, they would try to squirm away if she bent to pick them up, and soon she no longer even tried.

There are many dangers facing lion cubs, quite apart from infanticide and the threat of other predators. In 1998, we filmed a cub being killed by buffaloes and its mother later eating it. We debated the pros and cons of showing this incident. We all felt we should, without making it seem gratuitous. Taken out of context, a mother eating her own cub could seem macabre, yet for a lioness it was the most natural thing to do. George Schaller commented on witnessing such an incident that at least the lioness was able to recoup in some small way her investment in the life of her cub. He had witnessed infanticide when a new coalition of male lions found three cubs hidden beneath a fallen tree and killed them all. The lions carried off two of the dead cubs, leaving the third one where it lay. Schaller waited for the mother to return. 'At dusk she came. I was not certain what to expect, certainly not a wild expression of grief, but perhaps some sentiment. Instead she ate the cub, and as I sat there in the dark listening to her crunch the bones of her offspring, I could only conclude that it is difficult for man to return in imagination to the simplicity of a lion's outlook.'

The Topi Plains males now systematically hunted down Khali and her remaining cubs. Angie and I waited with her one morning as the males once again crested the rise separating the Topi Plains from the Marsh Lions' territory. Scar had already seen the

*O*f all the animals that lions prey on, buffaloes are the most likely to injure them – even when the lions are not interested in hunting; hardly surprising when one considers how important buffaloes are as prey to many prides. On this occasion a small bachelor herd of bull buffaloes surprised Khali as she lay suckling her cubs in the open at the edge of the Bila Shaka lugga. Scar and some of the older generation of cubs, including Khali's son and daughter, lay in a huddle alongside mother and babies. As soon as the buffaloes spotted the lions they lumbered towards them, noses in the air, grunting, intent on seeing off the pride. Scar and the older cubs scattered, leaving Khali stranded in the open – it is every lion for itself in circumstances such as this. The cubs tried to follow the rest of the pride, but were slowed down by the tangle of long grass as they scrambled to reach the lugga. Khali turned to face the buffaloes, bravely attempting to deflect the lumbering charge of the leading bull, trying to draw him away to give her cubs time to escape. But the buffaloes were too canny to be taken in by that kind of deception. They could smell the cubs in the long grass, hear their pathetic cries of distress. The lead bull wheeled around and rammed his boss into the ground, then with a flick of his massive horns tossed a cub high in the air, ripping a hole in its side and killing it instantly. At one point Khali was almost nose to nose with the bulls, distracting them sufficiently that the other three cubs managed to escape in all the mayhem, hiding in the croton thickets until the danger had passed. When the buffaloes had gone, Khali retrieved the dead cub and carried it in her mouth to the bushes. Angie had long since identified each of the cubs and knew this to be the smallest of the litter. Khali lay there licking it for a while, calling with that soft 'augh' sound lionesses use when they are trying to attract their cubs' attention and want them to come here or follow. Then she ate it.

Khali came within inches of being tossed by the buffaloes, bravely defending her cubs from attack. Scar meanwhile kept a safe distance among the croton thickets. Less than 20 per cent of cubs reach maturity; the rest fall victim to starvation, desertion, infanticide, predation or incidents such as this.

Though three of Khali's cubs managed to escape, the fourth was tossed high in the air and mortally wounded, horned through the chest.

Khali carries her dead cub to the Bila Shaka lugga where, after licking it for a while, she ate it, a not unexpected reaction for a carnivore.

Scar, Khali, her two-year-old daughter (sleeping) and the young cubs resting at the edge of the Bila Shaka lugga, moments before the pride was attacked by a herd of buffaloes.

males coming and had crossed the Bila Shaka lugga. He stood and roared. Was he hoping that Scruffy might suddenly come charging to the rescue, as he had so often done in the past, or that the rest of the pride would appear and help him repel the invaders? Khali had little option but to stay close to her cubs, who continued playing at the edge of the lugga as she stared into the distance, never taking her eyes from the males. At one point she began moving towards them, baring her teeth and hissing – a defensive gesture used by lions when faced with a threat that they cannot easily combat by outright aggression. The cubs realized from their mother's response that danger was afoot, and disappeared down the nearest warthog burrow. When she was

sure it was safe, Khali called the cubs to her, and then turned and headed in the direction of the marsh, stopping every so often to look back over her shoulder at the males. Fortunately the grass was long enough to shield the cubs from them.

On this occasion, we couldn't even be certain if the males had seen Khali; they were too intent on following Scar and chasing him away again. We watched as he ran for his life, barely keeping ahead of the two blond males as they chased him up and over the open plains to the north until he was well beyond the limits of his territory. At one point the bigger male closed with Scar, reaching out with claws bared to swat at his backside. But Scar just kept running, a trail of urine betraying his fear. Satisfied

for the moment, the males turned and hurried back to the lugga. Even if they hadn't seen Khali, they quickly picked up her scent. They prowled around the tall reeds in the floor of the lugga where she had hidden her cubs for the last few days in a muddy depression. The males sniffed and curled their lips in a flehmen face, testing the scent. They certainly would have recognized the smell of young cubs – cubs which did not have the scent of their own pride and which they would kill if they could find them. But on this occasion Khali had managed to escape.

Eventually the males must have caught up with Khali. When we next saw her a few months later the cubs had disappeared and she was mating with the older of the Topi

Plains males, while her pride mate consorted with the younger male. And so the age-old cycle of renewal continued, with one coalition of males being replaced by another. For Khali there was the chance of raising a new litter of cubs. It mattered less who sired her cubs than who could best protect them.

Scar now faced an uncertain future. He was probably about nine or ten years old, and might survive a while longer by staying close to his young relatives in the marsh. If not he would be forced into exile, wandering through the acacia thickets to the north of the reserve where Scruffy had been killed, though trying to avoid a similar fate might prove difficult. The temptation for a hungry lion to kill livestock was all too real and Scar's luxuriant ginger mane would be a fine trophy for a group of young warriors.

Life for a lion is full of life-and-death encounters. The takeovers by new males and the killing of cubs, the wars with buffaloes and hyenas may all appear dramatic and unusual to the human observer, yet they are a normal part of a lion's existence. I am sure some people feel uncomfortable with the fact that we are unable to interfere when things go wrong for the animal stars of *Big Cat Diary*. But nature has its own balances, and wild places depend for their unique character on non-interference by people. Predator and prey have evolved over eons, each refined by the process: the predator sublime in its hunting skills, the prey a picture of perfection as it runs and jumps to avoid being eaten. Buffalo calves are killed by lions, and lion cubs killed by buffaloes. Only by becoming big, strong and aggressive are buffaloes able to match the collective power of a pride of lions. And only by becoming social and co-operating can lions kill prey as large as this. That is the way of the wild.

Khali with her cubs on the morning when the Topi Plains males appeared along the Bila Shaka lugga. A single lioness can do little to protect her young cubs from infanticide – one reason why being part of a crèche and raising cubs communally is such an advantage.

# The Marsh Sisters

Though modern lions are thought to have adopted a social way of life relatively recently, they weren't the first big cats to do so. It seems certain that some of the extinct species of cats formed groups. The North American lion, *Panthera leo atrox*, probably hunted adult bison in this way, and sabre-toothed cats such as *Smilodon* and *Homotherium* – both lion-sized – would have benefited from joining forces to prey on juvenile mammoths and bison.

The modern lion's solitary relatives – the tiger, jaguar and leopard – all tend to live in more wooded environments or forests, which allow a single stalking cat to get close to its prey and favour a primarily solitary existence, with adults coming together for mating and little else. Because these cats are able to overpower their prey alone – and generally don't hunt such large animals as lions do – they have no need to form groups; and avoiding contact with one another helps to reduce competition for living space. Too many individuals hunting in the same area would be liable to disturb their prey and make it more difficult for any one cat to hunt successfully. Under these circumstances a solitary system of land tenure works best.

By contrast, lions are often found in open terrain composed of grasslands with scattered trees, in savanna woodlands or in semi-arid regions, where larger prey is abundant (though dispersed) and often clumped together in herds, requiring the predators to maintain large territories. Co-operation in hunting and rearing young would seem the most efficient way for lions to live, and among the carnivores in general the species that hunt in groups are the most social, such as the wolf, wild dog and hyena. The life expectancy for individuals of any of these species is greatly reduced if they are forced to live on their own, and the same applies to lions.

But just how different are lions from other members of the genus *Panthera*? If you scratch beneath the surface of their distinctive coats it would take an expert to

Half-Tail the leopard. Leopards are the most adaptable of the cat family and the most numerous of the world's big cats.

tell a lion from a tiger; their skeletons are very similar in size and appearance, though they can be distinguished by their skulls. Seen in the wild, lions appear higher at the shoulder than tigers and have shorter necks; in fact the shape and posture of the lion are closer to that other plains-dwelling cat, the cheetah. Experts believe that the lion's ancestor lived in the forests, and probably had similar markings to jaguars and

leopards, and that the move into more open habitat is relatively recent. In fact the coats of young lion cubs are dappled with spots and rosettes, hinting at this spotted ancestor. These markings fade as the cubs mature, though some adult lions maintain them along the sides of their bellies and the margins of their legs.

Investigations into the roaring abilities of the big cats also underline the close

relationship between lions, leopards and jaguars. You have only to listen to a leopard's contact call, a repeated series of rasping coughs, to recognize elements of the lion's magnificent roar as it tails off into a series of grunts. Tigers make a very different sound: single roars repeated every so often, but not in the well-defined sequence characteristic of lions and leopards.

Coat colour and patterning certainly seem to serve the different species of cats well in merging with their surroundings and enhancing their ability to avoid detection by their prey and their enemies. But this cannot be the only reason. In areas where black or melanistic leopards occur, such as the Aberdare National Park in Kenya, they blend with the sunlight and shadows of the forests as easily as the commoner spotted

forms. And tigers and leopards co-exist (though not on a friendly basis – tigers kill leopards when they can) in the forests of India, despite having very different coat markings. George Schaller has provided us with a persuasive explanation: that the markings help individuals of the same species to recognize one another from a distance. Apart from lessening the risk of conflict, this would serve to reduce the likelihood of hybridization in areas where species overlap, such as those parts of India where lions, tigers and leopards all occur. This theory is supported by the fact that big cats with similar markings, such as lions and pumas or jaguars and leopards, do not occur together.

Though lions, leopards and tigers are hostile in their dealings with one another in the wild, the differences in behaviour of the

Lion cubs (almost one year old) drinking from Lake Lagarja on the southern boundary of the Serengeti. Young lions have spots and rosettes, hinting at a forest-living, leopard-like ancestor.

Half-Tail's daughter Shadow. A female leopard spends much of her adult life either pregnant or in the company of one to three cubs.

Lions roar mostly at night and can be heard for 5km (3 miles) or more, with a male's roar being deeper and louder than a lioness's.

social lion and its solitary relatives may be more real than apparent, and may provide clues as to how lions became social. Certainly leopards and tigers are not as strictly anti-social as the word 'solitary' might imply, and female cats spend much of their lives in the company of dependent cubs with whom they socialize to varying degrees until they are almost fully grown. Though adult male and female leopards tend to avoid each other most of the time, males move around their territory on a regular basis and get to know the different females in their area, checking for fresh scent deposited on rocks and bushes, and learning to recognize the individual call and scent of each female living there. Males do sometimes meet up with a female and her cubs, and – as with tigers – have been observed interacting amicably with young

cubs that they have sired. How frequent these meetings are is uncertain, as they often occur at night. It could be that the male is attracted to the female's scent when she has young cubs, and males occasionally even mate with females long before the previous generation of cubs have become independent. Such meetings probably encourage a sense of ownership on the part of the male – a sense of 'his females' and 'his cubs' – and may heighten his efforts to keep the area secure.

Leopards are sometimes seen within view of one another in the vicinity of a kill – as are male and female tigers – and given the opportunity a male will scavenge food from a kill made by a female, or vice versa, though they stop short of feeding together. But then leopards primarily kill prey that is smaller than themselves, and even the

social lion is reluctant to share small prey with its pride mates. The fact that young female leopards generally try to stay on in the area where they were born and overlap part of their mother's home range (while avoiding each other) is also of significance, and somewhat similar to the pattern adopted by young lionesses when they are forced to leave their natal pride but choose to remain on the periphery of its territory. So the divisions between a solitary existence and a social one are not as distinct as they might appear, implying a degree of flexibility in the behaviour of leopards and tigers with the potential under different circumstances of evolving further.

Certainly when the forests began to open up millions of years ago it provided the opportunity for the evolution of a big cat adapted to hunt the wide variety of large prey found in more open habitats. Any lion wanting to pull down an animal as big as a full-grown buffalo or giraffe needs help, though a lioness hunting on her own will not hesitate to take on an animal the size of a full-grown wildebeest or zebra, and often succeeds in killing it. But this is far more food than a single lion can eat.

Whatever the factors might be that have fashioned lion society, spotted hyenas must have played a part in it. Any time lions make a large kill, it is liable to attract unwanted attention. If there are hyenas in the vicinity – and there certainly will be in places such as the Mara and Serengeti – then it may not be long before a lioness is forced to abandon her kill, unless she is a member of a pride and other lions are close at hand to help keep the hyenas at bay. Studies in Botswana have shown that small groups of lionesses, and prides without males, often struggle to defend their kills against large clans of hyenas. The balance

of power is generally one lioness to four hyenas, so lionesses in a small group could easily find themselves outnumbered in areas with high densities of hyenas. But most significantly, whenever male lions were present – even if it was only one – the hyenas were rarely able to drive the lions off their kill until they had filled their stomachs, leaving only the skin and bones for the powerful jaws of the hyenas to finish off.

We can only guess at what the ancestral lion might have looked like – a lynx-like creature perhaps, living a solitary existence in somewhat open country. By tolerating her adult daughters – possibly grudgingly at first – the female of the species might have opened the door to a more social way of life, in which she and her female relatives pooled their resources in defending their young and protecting large food items from hyenas. This in turn would have prompted male lions to form groups, and led to

young male relatives staying together when they left their natal pride. Once this process had started it would have been to the lions' advantage to form large groups to counter the tendency of neighbours to try and control as much territory as possible.

When I first started watching lions in the Mara, I was under the impression that while all young males were forced from their natal pride, their sisters and female cousins stayed on. But by following the Marsh Lions over the years I discovered that this was not always the case. A lioness gives birth to cubs every two years if the previous litter survives, and continues to breed most of her life. Under these circumstances there is often already a full complement of lionesses in the pride when the next generation of young females matures, in which case they are forced out. The fact that every two or three years new males move in and oust the resident males plays a role in this process, as quite apart from killing any small cubs the males expel the subadults too – and not just the young males. Subadult females aren't yet ready to mate and would compete for food with any cubs that the new males might sire. Suddenly all the security that these young females have enjoyed as members of a pride is denied them, and unless they are fortunate enough to be part of a large group of exiles they are likely to struggle to survive.

Females do sometimes manage to establish a territory of their own away from their natal territory. Depending on how strong the group is they may even displace their older female relatives and force them to eke out a living in less ideal habitat. Over the years we have watched various groups of young Marsh females stubbornly resisting the efforts of their older relatives to drive them away, even attempting to raise their cubs along the Bila Shaka lugga, close to where they were born. But the time usually comes when the pressure of too many lions in too little space becomes intolerable, and either the youngsters or

A single lioness has less success than a group in hunting zebras, because a zebra's fierce kick can break a lioness's jaw. If this happens, a lioness who has no pride mates to share their food with her may starve to death.

The presence of pride males at a kill makes it virtually impossible for any number of hyenas to steal the carcass.

their older relatives move out of the core area. In fact within a year or so of my coming to live in the Mara, the group of four adult Marsh lionesses I had been watching nurse their cubs at Bila Shaka were forced to give ground to five young females who had been exiled from the pride as three-year-olds. After a period of roaming around the periphery of their old haunts and a number of spats with other groups of lions, these lionesses forced a show-down with their relatives, culminating in a noisy cat fight near the marsh. From that time onwards it was the five younger females whom we would find patrolling the marsh or lying confidently among the croton bushes of the Bila Shaka lugga, and it was the group of mature lionesses who looked nervous and harassed whenever we found them. Before long the oldest of them had disappeared and eventually the pride died out from lack of numbers, though an element of continuity remained, as the area was still occupied by a group of females

who were descended from the original Marsh Pride.

Small groups of lionesses rarely manage to make the transition to owning a well-defined territory, though they may survive

for years on their own or in twos and threes. These females live their lives as refugees among the established prides, constantly forced on their way again, trying as best they can to avoid endless scraps

Hyenas have incredibly powerful molar teeth, capable of chewing through a zebra's thigh bone to feed on the marrow.

Lionesses from the Big Pride grooming. The largest pride recorded in the Mara numbered 48 lions, although the average is just over twenty.

could find topis and zebras, shunning waterlogged terrain such as Musiara Marsh. But Red and Gimpy couldn't afford to be choosy, and we often found them skulking around the edges of the riverine forest bordering the marsh, near to the *Big Cat Diary* camp, hunting waterbucks, warthogs and the occasional impala.

Surprisingly, perhaps, whenever we met the Marsh Sisters they looked fit and

over food and living space. They sometimes bear the marks of serious injuries and in the all-important race to breed they are greatly disadvantaged. Life without sufficient pride members is a genetic dead-end, and a pride seldom flourishes unless it contains at least three adult females.

The Marsh Sisters were one such group, composed of two lionesses known as Red and Gimpy, who had been born to different mothers in the Marsh Pride about ten years ago. Red was a handsome lioness, big-bodied with a dark reddish-brown coat. She had a broad head and square jaw with a fierce look about her, reminding us of her mother Brown, who in her day had always been the first to lead an assault on intruders in Marsh Lion territory. Red was bigger than the lighter-coated Gimpy, more thick-set, and was one of our favourites.

When Red and Gimpy were about two and a half years old there were no openings in the Marsh Pride to allow them to stay on, no vacancies due to deaths and no other female relatives of a similar age to bolster their numbers when the time came

to leave. It was the arrival of new pride males that prompted the females to strike out on their own. Too young to mate with the males but old enough to keep out of harm's way, Red and Gimpy were forced to distance themselves from their older relatives. To add to their problems, Gimpy had the disadvantage of a withered hind leg, making her a yard or so slower in the chase than Red. But even on three good legs Gimpy often succeeded in catching herself a meal, and when times were really tough there was always the possibility that Red would make a large kill for them both to share.

Like generations of young lionesses before them, Red and Gimpy were determined to survive close to the area where they were born. This was the place they knew best. They kept out of trouble most of the time by listening to the roars of their relatives and moving on when necessary. It was like a game of hide and seek. During the rains the Marsh Pride invariably sought the higher ground to the north of the Bila Shaka lugga where they healthy, if a little harassed, and were certainly getting enough to eat most of the time. They were always at their best during the dry season, when hundreds of thousands of wildebeest and zebras poured into the Mara from the Serengeti, and the killing was easy for all the lions. But life was destined to become much more difficult for the Marsh Sisters once they were old enough to breed. Even though you will sometimes see a young lioness mating in her third year, they rarely conceive until they are around four. And when a lioness does become pregnant for the first time it is not uncommon for her to lose her cubs: like all cats, lions seem to benefit from experience. There are many dangers to avoid and sometimes a lioness chooses a bad location to give birth – one young female delivered her first cub on the main road leading into Governor's Camp.

Whenever Red and Gimpy came into oestrus either the Marsh males or groups of nomads would track them down and mate with them. On more than one occasion we witnessed one of them being harassed by females from the Marsh Pride when they came into season. When they are mating a courting couple often become rather localized in their movements, and this

Male impala at the edge of Musiara Marsh at dawn. During the rains, the marsh is often shrouded in mist at first light.

sometimes posed problems for the Marsh Sisters when the other females moved into the area. Fortunately for them, the aggressive presence of the pride male usually prevented the Marsh Lion females from attacking Red or Gimpy, though they tried. When a male is guarding an oestrus female, he rarely lets another lion or lioness anywhere near her, regardless of where she comes from. Once mating was over, however, the males would wander on their way again, rather than staying and defending the lionesses and their future offspring. A group of just two females, such as Gimpy and Red, never seemed enough to encourage males to remain loyal to them, not in the Mara at least. The males were always on the look-out for new and

better opportunities to breed with larger groups of females.

Perhaps the fact that the Marsh Sisters were unable to stay in any one place all year round made it more difficult for them to attract resident males. They had a territory of sorts in as much as they would attack and chase away any young females who tried to move into the marsh, but it was more transitory than permanent. Whenever the Marsh Pride wanted to use the area, Red and Gimpy had to give way. Their life was a merry-go-round of getting pregnant, giving birth and then struggling to raise their cubs. Inevitably new males would find and kill their offspring, or the cubs simply couldn't keep up and the whole cycle would begin again. Rarely did

we see the females with large litters, and when we did we could only watch helplessly as one by one the cubs disappeared. There was just no permanence to the Marsh Sisters' lives.

Watching Red and Gimpy in their struggle to breed, we wondered why they never adopted the strategy employed by some nomadic males and forged an alliance with non-relatives to create a group large enough to hold a well-defined territory. Craig Packer, who for the last 20 years has headed the Serengeti Lion Project, puts it this way, 'Why associate only with family or with no one at all? There is no queen enforcing sterility on her subordinate kin, like termites or naked mole-rats.'

In fact, there are only two cases on

Defassa waterbucks. It is said that lions don't like eating waterbuck flesh, but they certainly try to kill them when they are hungry.

record of solitary lionesses joining up with non-relatives to form permanent prides in the Serengeti, and in both cases they had been forced to abandon their original ranges due to severe drought or human disruption. In other words it takes a lot to force a cat to leave an area with which it has become familiar, which is marked with its own scent and that of relatives, and which looks and feels like home. Lions mature slowly and by the time they are fully grown they know their natal territory intimately. Good lion country is going to have lots of adult lions competing for territories and quite ready to react aggressively to any young lions trying to settle. Young lionesses looking for a new range are liable to be tolerated by their relatives to a greater degree than by other prides of lions – at least until the time comes to breed – and this is another strong incentive for sticking close to home. As Packer says, 'Allowing the kids to camp in the backyard may not guarantee them a successful start in life, but it provides them with a safe refuge until a neighbour's house goes on the market.'

In the early days we had thought that maybe, just maybe, Red and Gimpy might one day manage to rejoin the Marsh Pride. Was it possible that they would be recognized as kin and accepted back when older lionesses died or were killed? But when divisions occur between female pride members, they are almost always permanent. Lions seem to have short memories and I have often thought that scent seems equally as important as visual recognition – if not more so – in identifying who belongs in the pride. When a lioness returns to where other pride members are resting after absenting herself on some outing, she may be stalked in a most threatening way by her companions, as if they are unsure who she is. Only when she is very close and maintains a confident approach and bearing, acknowledging that this is her place too, does the tension suddenly evaporate into a playful embrace

Red, one of the Marsh Sisters, carrying a cub of about two to three weeks old. A lioness frequently moves her cubs during the first few weeks.

and greeting, with the lionesses rubbing heads and sniffing under each other's tails to verify who is who.

Lions are well endowed with scent glands, situated on their heads, chins, the corners of their mouths, in the anal region and between their toes. Exchanging scent by rubbing and sniffing helps to bond pride members together and create a pride scent. But once lionesses are separated for more than a few months, former allies become rivals for the rest of their lives. Craig Packer cites just one example of two female relatives who managed to overcome their deeply ingrained hostility to one another and were reunited after years of living apart. But even together, by the age of ten they had never raised cubs. Little wonder that if lionesses are so resistant to joining up again with relatives, they almost never team up with non-relatives, despite the obvious benefits that they would enjoy if they did.

Imagine our shock, then, when one morning we found a group of females that we didn't recognize walking towards a branch of the Bila Shaka lugga. Then we noticed that one of them was limping. We checked our records and sure enough it was Gimpy and her daughter Go-Cat. After years of struggling, Gimpy had finally managed to raise a single female cub, a rather nervous youngster who was now a year and a half old. But none of us had any idea who the other females were, though the fact that they didn't react aggressively meant that they knew one another even if we didn't know them. Perhaps they were two generations of exiles from the Marsh Pride who had fed or scavenged from the same kill made in no-man's land. We never discovered the answer to that question. But when we next saw Gimpy and Go-Cat they were back at the marsh and Red was with them.

"*Not long ago I wrote in my journal: Today we were particularly keen to catch up with a small group of lionesses known as the Marsh Sisters, who have been forced from the Marsh Pride as three-year-olds and had struggled for years to eke out an existence on the fringes of the Marsh Pride's territory.*

*During our absence, Red, the oldest lioness, had given birth to four cubs in a thicket close to the edge of Musiara Marsh. We met her one morning moving the tiny cubs from their scent-soiled den to a new hiding place barely 100m away. Red broke into a trot as the last of the cubs cried out in protest at being abandoned so abruptly by its mother and siblings. Gimpy and Go-Cat watched from the top of a nearby termite mound, and we couldn't help but marvel at the tenacity of these females; the way they simply refused to be cowed by their circumstances. Red's cubs are still too small to recognize individually, but their whisker spots will soon be distinct enough for us to record.*

*Life will always be tough for such a small pride. Starvation, predation, nomadic male lions and battles with other females for territory are all potent killers of lion cubs, with 50 per cent or less surviving to adulthood. This is not Red's first litter of cubs, but it is a new beginning. Angie and I can only hope for better times for Red and her fellow Marsh Sisters.*"

One of the Marsh Sisters' favourite resting places was a clump of croton bushes on a rocky rise overlooking the marsh. This is a good vantage point for the lionesses to keep an eye out for trouble, whether it be the approach of other lions or the Masai coming to water their cattle at the spring. And it is close enough to the reed-beds to set up an ambush if prey is in the area. On one occasion we found Red, Gimpy and Go-Cat feeding on a zebra carcass concealed in long grass. They looked nervous, as if expecting trouble, and one or other of them would keep sitting up and looking around, before burying her face in the carcass again. Eventually a single hyena picked up the scent of offal and with its head low to the ground began to call – a series of long-drawn-out whoops that carried far out into the plains. In no time more than a dozen hyenas had come running to investigate. At one point lions and hyenas lay flanked on either side of the carcass; the lions too hungry to waste valuable time trying to chase the mob away, the hyenas intent on bolting down all the food they could manage before more of their kind arrived.

Suddenly the hyenas scattered as a big male lion galloped into their midst, blond mane flowing, grunting as he ran. It was one of the Topi Plains males, who with his younger companion was now ensconced as undisputed ruler of the Marsh Pride. The three lionesses bolted, and just in time. Khali, Bump Nose and other members of the Marsh Pride had heard the noisy squabbling of the hyena clan and knew that there was a kill in their territory. While the blond male dragged the zebra carcass into the lugga, the Marsh lionesses stood and roared in the direction of their relatives, hurrying the Marsh Sisters on their way. It was a graphic example of the power of numbers; of how in open country living in a group is the best way to survive; and how small groups are always at a disadvantage in defending a kill – or a hunting territory – against larger numbers of lions and hyenas. And it bore witness to the fact that hyenas are most easily kept at bay when you have pride males on your side. Though in this case the females did not benefit from the male's presence as he finished off the carcass on his own.

A lion can consume up to a quarter of its body weight at a sitting, and though lions tend to hunt every few days, they can go for long periods without food if need be.

Hyenas have great endurance and are coursers like wild dogs, keeping up a steady gallop for kilometre after kilometre. They have very acute senses of hearing and smell, and can detect a kill from kilometres away.

It was not to be. Once again Red lost her cubs, though more recently Gimpy gave birth to a new litter and was seen on a number of occasions near the marsh with two cubs of about nine weeks old. Then disaster struck. The Marsh Sisters had always lived a precarious existence on the edge of the reserve. Inevitably they sometimes came into contact with the Masai and their livestock, and on one occasion during the prolonged drought Red was seen to attack a cow that had become separated from the herd. Before she could dispatch her victim, David Breed, who drives Simon King's camera car when we are filming *Big Cat Diary*, raced across to where Red had pulled down the cow. Though Red was reluctant to abandon her victim, Dave managed to scare her off before she could suffocate the cow – just as a Masai herdsman came running over, spear raised. On that occasion Red's life was spared. But not this time.

Friends of fellow wildlife photographers Joe and Mary Ann McDonald, who had witnessed the incident, took up the story. Both lionesses looked thin and that Red was lactating. One of the lionesses had killed a calf about a kilometre (two-thirds of a mile) north of the boundary and had dragged it into a thicket where both began feeding. A few hundred metres (yards) away a herdboy stood watching with his cattle, and at first Joe and Mary Ann thought that all would be well. But the word had already gone out to the surrounding villages. Before long, some 30 red-robed Masai men and teenage boys came running; armed with their long spears and their simis – the short, stabbing sword that every Masai carries and uses in close combat. On they came to where the calf had been killed. Gimpy fled first, perhaps aware of the handicap of her deformed leg, but Red was desperate for food and continued feeding for a few more seconds. She had got away with it before. But this time there was no holding the Masai back. The death of the cow had to be avenged; it was justice to the Masai, their culture dictated it. Nobody would compensate them for their loss, and it was up to them to ensure that it didn't happen too often.

They trapped Red in dense bush bordering the lugga where she had gone to ground. Surrounded by 20 men there was no escape. Red roared out in terror and pain as the first spear hit home. Within seconds she was dead. The Masai who had thrown the first spear cut off her tail and held it above his head. That was his right, his badge of honour. I remember my good friend Jim Cavanaugh, who has been watching the Nairobi Park lions on a daily basis for some years, remarking how easy it was to spear a cornered lion. In the old days the Masai would protect themselves by carrying buffalo-hide shields as tall as a man when they went to war or on a lion hunt. As the lion tried to break from cover it would focus all its fear and fury on the individual nearest to it, who would crouch behind his shield as the lion charged. Once the first spear had found its mark the other warriors moved like lightning to finish the lion off. Jim was shattered to witness such an incident in the Kitengela, bordering Nairobi Park, as he begged the herdsmen to spare the life of a lion who had left the park to find food and had taken to stock-raiding. But neither words nor money would sway them.

Perhaps it is too much to ask the Masai – or anyone else – to sacrifice their livelihood to preserve wildlife outside protected areas, particularly when they feel that they see few benefits from the tourist's dollar. As I thought about the death of Red, I was reminded of how far man has distanced himself from the predators. Thanks to language and strategy – co-operation in the hunt – man can now so easily outwit a lion and neutralize its power. Living as part of a group serves the individual so much better than trying to go it alone – for lions and for humans. Gimpy and her two young cubs may have survived the incident, but their future looked bleaker than ever now that Red was gone.

# The Serengeti Lion

Mara and Serengeti are one land. Empire-builders may have given them a separate identity when they carved up East Africa, but they are still inextricably linked by the passage of the wandering herds of wildebeest and zebras. The great migration defines the extent of this 25,000km² (10,000sq. mile) ecosystem, the last wild place on earth where you can see so many animals gathered together. The diversity of life makes it a predator's paradise and, though much smaller than the Serengeti, the Mara is vital to the migration as a dry-season refuge. But it is the Serengeti that has dominated the public's view of Africa, ever since those pioneering Germans Bernhard and Michael Grzimek filmed and wrote *Serengeti Shall Not Die*, which

attained a worldwide audience in the late 1950s. Serengeti is easy on the eye and as much as anywhere has come to represent the quintessential African landscape: open plains dotted with flat-topped acacias, a pride of lions recumbent in the shade.

When I first visited the Serengeti in 1974, George Schaller had already published the findings of his landmark study in *The Serengeti Lion*. I was lucky enough to see lions, leopards and cheetahs during that first fleeting visit, and Schaller's book acted as the bible of big cat behaviour, allowing me to interpret my own observations as I embarked on my fledgling career as a big-cat watcher. That three-day safari during my overland trip through Africa left me aching for the opportunity to

live and work in the bush. Little did I realize that it would be the last I saw of the Serengeti's wide-open spaces and acacia woodlands for nearly ten years. In an attempt to reclaim its tourist industry, Tanzania closed its border with Kenya in 1977, the year I arrived to live in the Mara and immerse myself in the world of the Marsh Lions. It was only after the border had closed that the Mara assumed its rightful place in the public's mind as one of the world's great wildlife areas; prior to that it had been little more than an overnight stop for many visitors to East Africa as they headed back to Nairobi after visiting Ngorongoro Crater and the Serengeti.

Each year in early June, the first cavalcades of wildebeest and zebras arrive

Young males in Kruger often become 'floaters' rather than true nomads, wandering close to where they were born until they are big enough to take over a pride.

in the Mara, crossing an intermittent watercourse known as the Sand River that marks the boundary with the Serengeti. When the herds slipped away again with the onset of the rains in October, I longed to accompany them south to the short-grass plains. This is the ancestral home of the migration, where the cow wildebeest give birth to 400,000 calves each year and where Schaller had watched nomadic lions grow fat on the proceeds of nature's profligacy.

Lions living in the Mara and Serengeti form a single population, and the nomads among them know no boundaries, covering huge distances as they travel back and forth in search of a place to live, relying on the one and a half million wildebeest and zebras for sustenance. Some of these wandering males eventually manage to find a pride of females that they can take over, and whenever new males emerged to wrest

control of the Marsh Pride's territory I couldn't help wondering how far they had travelled to make their conquest, and whether they might not be Serengeti males.

As the migratory herds return to the Serengeti many of the nomadic lions follow them, unless they have managed to find a territory. Almost half the pride takeovers in Serengeti occur in November and December as the wildebeest and zebras return, and females who have lost cubs to infanticide, or do not have them at all, soon come into oestrus and mate with the new males, though they generally don't become pregnant for up to three months. This 'pseudo-oestrus' is thought to be nature's way of ensuring that the females end up with the best mates. There may be more than one coalition of males in the area at the time of a takeover, and if the females immediately became pregnant they might find that another coalition had taken

control by the time their cubs were born; then the whole cycle of infanticide and social disruption would begin all over again. Better to allow the male groups to establish which is the strongest coalition, and only then ovulate and become pregnant with their offspring. Mating with the males is safer than being injured or even killed for not being receptive.

Though lionesses give birth at any time of the year, there does seem to be a seasonal peak in the Serengeti between March and July. This may be partly due to the earlier upsurge in pride takeovers, and also to the fact that, thanks to the abundance of food, lionesses tend to reach peak physical condition at this time of year and come into season more often. Hence most pregnancies or suckling of small cubs occur when the migration is in the area.

Until relatively recently, whenever people spoke about lions they were talking about a

River crossings are always a dangerous time for the herds, providing the opportunity for crocodiles and lions to ambush them.

creature shaped in our imagination by the behaviour of the Serengeti lion. Only in the last decade have scientists working in other parts of Africa begun to challenge our view of these majestic cats and highlighted the way lions behave in different kinds of habitats. Even so, for the past 36 years the Serengeti Lion Project has been the mainstay of lion research in Africa. Together with the chimpanzee study pioneered by Jane Goodall at Tanzania's Gombe National Park, it is one of the longest-running research projects on a large mammal anywhere in the world. It is a remarkable tribute to the quality of George Schaller's work that the seeds of much of what has been substantiated about lion behaviour throughout Africa date back to his study.

Over the years the Serengeti Lion Project has evolved from determining the numbers of lions and their range size and providing a broad outline of their behaviour, to embrace the latest techniques in computer modelling and genetics. Each Serengeti lion has an identification card showing its whisker-spot pattern and every time a lion reappears its ID card is updated: where was it seen, who was it with, what condition was it in and how well fed was it? Many of the lions have been followed from birth to death, allowing the researchers to chronicle their life histories and, with the help of DNA fingerprinting, map out the precise relationship of individuals within a pride. Nearly 3,000 lions have been studied in Serengeti and the Ngorongoro Crater. But trying to make sense of the way lions live is never-ending. When Craig Packer and his wife Ann Pusey took over the Lion Project in 1978, they were particularly interested to explore lion sociality.

Some of the possible benefits of group living had already been identified, with acquiring food high on the list. Also included were the capture of larger prey, minimizing the risk of starvation for individual pride members, making it easier to hunt and capture animals in widely dispersed herds and defending kills from

A Marsh lioness tries to pull down an orphaned elephant calf. No species is immune to attack from hungry lions; giraffes, crocodiles and rhino calves are all taken at times.

spotted hyenas, thereby maximizing the amount of food eaten from each carcass. Living in a group should also reduce the risk of predation: the animal that hunts or forages on its own has a greater chance of becoming someone else's meal. Though lions have no natural predators to fear as adults – apart from man – they do face serious competition from animals that might kill them – specifically, other lions.

It was evident to Packer and Pusey that lions formed larger groups than would be expected based purely on finding enough to eat. One of the pivotal assumptions about a lion pride is that the lionesses are related and that they are intolerant of non-relatives intruding on their territory. Offering group membership to a relative would prevent her from suffering the consequences of foraging on her own. Under these circumstances it seemed reasonable to expect lions to remain in groups, unless the group grew to the point that any one kill had to feed so many mouths that an individual hunter could have done better for herself.

Most carnivores are solitary, and those that aren't – spotted hyenas and wild dogs as well as lions – have always been thought to have adopted a social way of life primarily because it yielded greater success in hunting. All three species have seized the opportunity of living in more open habitats, providing access to larger prey than most solitary species of predators can handle. Both male and female hyenas and wild dogs participate in group hunts. But in the Mara and Serengeti it is lionesses who do most of the hunting, and so it seemed likely that the driving force behind lion sociality was the benefit of co-operative hunting for the females.

Lions are versatile predators, particularly when you take into account how big they are. A hungry lion will hunt just about anything, from insects, reptiles, birds, hares and gazelle fawns to animals as large as giraffes and even young elephants. But despite their reputation as consummate hunters, there are many occasions when lions are forced to abandon a stalk long before they come within striking distance, and even when they do attack they manage to kill only about once in every five attempts. Not surprisingly they scavenge as much as they can and where prey and other predators are plentiful 50 per cent of their food may come from scavenging. During

Schaller's time in the Serengeti he found that lionesses hunting co-operatively in groups of five or six were twice as successful in catching prey (30 per cent success rate) as a lioness hunting alone (15 per cent success rate), seeming to confirm that the principal impetus for pride formation was increased hunting success. Schaller described the situation most likely to yield success as being 'for a group of lions to stalk a solitary large animal upwind near a thicket at night'. But this was based primarily on data involving lions hunting wildebeest, zebras and Thomson's gazelles – migratory species. Prior to Schaller's study, people had always assumed that lions 'understood' the importance of wind direction on the outcome of a hunt. But having watched hundreds of hunts and recorded the wind direction, Schaller found that lions did not take this into account and regularly suffered the consequences when they approached from upwind and the prey picked up their scent.

One undisputed benefit of hunting in a group is that it sometimes allows lions to make multiple kills, providing all pride members with the chance to eat their fill. We often witnessed this while watching the Marsh Lions hunting wildebeest during the dry season, and saw them encircle a herd as it began to get dark, with each lioness creeping forward until one of them made a move and the herd scattered, enabling the lions to overpower two or three animals, and hinting at a degree of co-operation. On one occasion we counted four wildebeest of various ages lying dead in the grass, some of them untouched. Obviously this is not something that a single lioness can do, though a lone hunter does sometimes kill a wildebeest and then given the chance later pick off another – and another – from the same ambush site.

The reason for this seemingly excessive killing is that in all cats the hunting drive is independent of the hunger drive. How many times has one watched a domestic cat that has just been fed by its owner respond to the opportunity to hunt a garden bird? But in the wild, predators rarely get the chance to 'overkill', and even when they do nothing is wasted. The smaller predators and vultures soon finish off anything that the lions can't eat. A lion's life oscillates between times of plenty and times of hardship; it is a feast-or-famine regime with the lions never quite knowing when or from where the next meal is coming; better to eat as much as you can when you can and build up energy reserves for the inevitable lean times.

For lions living in the Serengeti–Mara, the arrival of the migration means that all the lions – regardless of group size – get plenty to eat. In fact lions build up body reserves during this period when prey is abundant, lactating females produce more milk and cubs rarely starve. Lionesses hunting on their own get as much to eat as those living in groups of any size, and for as long as wildebeest and zebras (and Thomson's gazelles in the Serengeti) are available, the lions feed almost exclusively on them. But there is no guarantee how long the animals will continue to stream into the area or how long they will stay. It may be for a week or a month; it all depends on the rains and the quality of the grazing. By being constantly on the move the migratory animals lessen the impact of predation: only by ranging widely can they survive in such vast numbers.

Male lions in East Africa weigh on average 175kg (385lb) and females 120kg (265lb); lions from southern Africa tend to be about 5 per cent larger. Though lionesses eat an average of about 6–8kg (13–18lb) per day, they can go without food for days – a week or more even – and on an empty stomach a female can eat 30kg (65lb) and a male close to 50kg (110lb) at a sitting – a quarter of their body weight. This means that each lion needs to kill about 20 medium-sized animals such as a wildebeest or topi each year, and a pride's territory is defined by how much food any given group of lions needs to survive year round. It has been suggested that high densities of prey weighing one to two times the weight of a lioness – such as a wildebeest or zebra – may have been a major factor in encouraging females to form prides, with

There are more than 35,000 vultures patrolling the skies over the Serengeti–Mara; the most numerous are the colonial white-backed vultures, seen here spreading their wings to cool themselves.

males prompted to join together in coalitions as the best way of controlling high densities of females concentrated into well-defined territories.

The crunch comes when the migration moves on. Then the lions have to work a lot harder to find sufficient food to sustain the pride. In lean times it is the cubs who suffer most, as they depend entirely on the lionesses for their next meal until they are almost two years old. A half-starved lioness will increasingly deny her cubs access to a kill if she is really hungry, simply because she can't afford to sacrifice her own life.

The Big Pride. Pride males sometimes allow their young cubs to feed on a carcass by keeping the lionesses at bay.

The wildebeest return to favoured crossing sites along the Mara River each year, generally choosing places with easy access to the river and good visibility.

Predators take a heavy toll on warthog piglets, which are frequently attacked by lions, hyenas, leopards, cheetahs and large birds of prey.

She can always breed again when times are better, something that cubs are too young to be able to do. Fortunately for the cubs, the pride males sometimes allow them to feed on a carcass while keeping the adult females at bay. This makes sense, as the cubs are related to at least one of the males, whereas the lionesses aren't related to any of them, and when cubs are small with small appetites the males can afford to be generous. This could mean the difference between life and death for the cubs, though when times are really hard they may get nothing and eventually die.

It is apparent when watching lions feeding on a kill that there is no social dominance among the females; every lion regardless of age or size will bite and slap when necessary to assert their right to a share. Jostling for access to a small kill such as a warthog may quickly degenerate into an unseemly fight, with the result that it is torn apart. This is often preceded by each lion holding on with all its might, not daring to release its portion to strike out at a rival for fear of losing its advantage. In these circumstances it is evident why lions have such big nostrils and nasal cavities: all the better to suck in air while their mouths are closed on a portion of meat or, more importantly, while strangling or suffocating their prey. A pride member who is fortunate enough to make a really small kill such as a warthog piglet or gazelle fawn is usually able to eat alone, though her cubs may try to claim a share. If another member of the group approaches, an aggressive snarl from the lioness in possession is usually enough to make her pride mate lie down or turn away; if not she can simply run off with her prize. But depending on how hungry they are, the pride males may try to steal even a small kill, and their size enables them to dominate females. They also generally consume twice as much from a carcass. If there are a number of lionesses feeding at a large kill, particularly if the males have eaten from it earlier, the males may be more cautious in their approach, lying and watching from a distance, and may wait until only one or two lionesses remain before appropriating the spoils.

Craig Packer still runs the Serengeti Lion Project from the University of Minnesota, where he and his wife are both professors, regularly returning to Tanzania to oversee the work of students. 'Co-operation in nature is rare, but lions, baboons and chimpanzees are among the most co-operative of all mammals,' says Packer, and he should know, having been involved in the study of all three species (both Packer and Pusey were students at Gombe National Park). But co-operation is always balanced against self-interest; helping invariably has its reward. How much did the grouping patterns shown by members of prides contribute to their success in obtaining food – was food really the reason for the way lions lived? Packer wasn't convinced. He had initially been confident that he could find the answers to his questions about lion social behaviour in just two or three years of intense field work. But he soon realized that only a long-term study could yield the information he was looking for. As he wryly commented, 'Lions are supremely adept at doing nothing. To the list of inert noble gases, including krypton, argon and neon, we could add lion.'

Single lions and smaller prides in the Serengeti–Mara rely heavily on warthogs when the migration is absent. Having stolen this kill from the lionesses, this pride male is about to allow the cubs to feed with him.

Packer, Pusey and their students have explored numerous avenues in an attempt to explain exactly why lions are social and what size of group brings the greatest benefits. Schaller had already identified the most obvious social activities lions engage in – group hunting, communal rearing of cubs in a crèche and group defence of a territory. And he had watched lions at night. But something still didn't add up.

Packer realized that only by watching known individuals 24 hours a day could he find what he was looking for. Beginning in 1984, at least one lioness in each of 21 prides was radio-collared, and Packer and one of his students, Dave Scheel, put themselves through a gruelling regime of night follows. They wanted to discover how much meat each female obtained, whether hunting alone or in a group. This meant following the lions day and night for four straight days around the time of a full moon, with the help of the radio-collared females and night-vision goggles. Packer and Scheel alternated six-hour shifts, with Packer taking the sunset-to-one-in-the-morning stint, and then taking over again at sunrise. True to form the lions slept most of the time, and the tension and boredom of it all took its toll on the human observers. Even now the thought of those long hours in the vehicle make Packer uneasy: 'I must admit that I still find it difficult to talk about this study. Each night alone in the car consisted largely of just trying to stay awake, trying to stay sane, coping with the endless, mindless soliloquy.'

They were forced to abandon several follows when the car broke down or fell in a pig hole, and one night Scheel came down with malaria. But they almost always managed to stay with the lions for the full four days, and completed 36 such follows in 24 months – 144 nights in the company of lions, with more than 1,500 sightings of radio-collared females between July 1984 and December 1987.

At the same time as Packer and Scheel were following the lions, I was working on a

Chacma baboon in South Luangwa National Park, Zambia. By forming large troops as a defence against predators, baboons are able to abandon the security of the trees and move into the open savannas to feed.

Even though wild dogs are coursers, they will bunch together and stalk as close as possible to prey in open country.

Thomson's gazelles are a favoured prey of wild dogs and cheetahs in the Serengeti–Mara. They give birth to their fawns during the rainy season, and typically come into oestrus within two weeks of calving, producing two calves in just over a year.

Gazelle fawns are easy for wild dogs and cheetahs to run down, so their only defence during the first few weeks of life is to lie out with their chins to the ground and remain motionless.

book on wild dogs and spent weeks sleeping out in my car so that I could stay with a pack when it established a den. This allowed me to watch the puppies during the first two months of their lives, and to keep track of the adults when they hunted early each morning and again in the evenings. But I was fortunate. The dogs rarely hunted at night, except when the moon was full, and having cooked myself some food on a gas stove I was able to crawl into the back of the car and fall asleep. I hardly needed a wake-up call. At first light the dogs would wander over and start tugging at the air nozzles protruding from the tyres or 'disembowel' the underside of the car, ripping at the electric wiring or fuel lines. Then they were off, breaking into that effortless stride of theirs, loping across the plains in search of gazelles or wildebeest. Whenever I bumped into Dave Scheel I was always amazed at how he managed to keep his sense of humour, let alone stay awake with his sleeping lions; it must have had something to do with the aura of the Serengeti. Everyone falls under its spell.

Wild dogs adopt a very different approach to lions when they decide to hunt. They are coursers, pursuing their prey until it becomes exhausted and then pulling it apart. Sometimes the dogs split up and chase individual members of a herd, but they quickly switch tack to take advantage of what other pack members are doing if they think it will increase their chance of gaining a meal. At times individuality is evident in ways that may benefit the pack. Certain dogs are particularly quick and adept at running down gazelles, others are more enduring in a chase after adult wildebeest, and some of the males are particularly skilled at leaping up to grab a struggling wildebeest or zebra by the lip and nose to immobilize it, allowing other members of the pack to pull it apart more easily. A pack's success rate, particularly when the wildebeest are calving on the plains, is high, and although they may make a number of attempts before they succeed in obtaining a meal, pack members rarely head back to the den with an empty stomach. When you watch a pack of wild dogs you are witnessing the height of social behaviour: all the adult males are related, and so too are all the females – though the sexes are not related to each other. No wonder 'helping' is such a feature of their lives, particularly when it comes to raising puppies.

Although lions can put on a frightening burst of speed (50–60 kph or 30–35mph) – as many a wild dog has found to its cost – they cannot sustain it for more than a few hundred metres, whereas a wild dog can keep up a similar pace for kilometre after kilometre. Spotted hyenas have equal stamina in the chase, and Schaller makes the point that a lion's heart is only 0.45 per cent of its body weight (a lioness's is slightly bigger at 0.57 per cent, but then they do most of the chasing), whereas a hyena's heart makes up almost 10 per cent of its body weight. Hunting success for a lion generally depends on getting as close to its prey as possible before bursting from cover; it quickly gives up as soon as the prey starts to pull away, unless a pride mate alters the outcome for the better.

Packer and Scheel's daunting work regime paid off. They discovered that during hard times in the Serengeti, solitary lionesses and lionesses living in small groups of two to four females tended to hunt warthogs more frequently than any other prey, just as they do in the Mara when prey is scarce. Warthogs are relatively small prey for lions, averaging 25–50kg (55–110lb), though a big male can weigh considerably more than this, and a solitary lioness proved just as likely to be successful hunting warthogs as a small group of lions. But because she didn't have to share her catch with companions, a solitary hunter obtained far more meat than a lioness working in a pair, trio or quartet. In fact during times of prey scarcity small groups were undernourished by comparison to solitary hunters, and might go for days without food. Solitary hunters and small groups scavenged up to 60 per cent of their food, while the larger prides gained virtually all of theirs from their own kills. Larger groups of five to seven lionesses tended to hunt buffaloes during lean times, and were as well fed as single lionesses – but no more so. Hardly surprisingly, then, warthogs and buffaloes accounted for 50 per cent of kills made by lions when times were difficult. One of the reasons that small groups of lionesses were the most disadvantaged was that they rarely hunted buffaloes. They had little choice in this: buffaloes are just too dangerous for a small group to attack. Meanwhile, the larger groups actively hunted buffaloes and reaped the benefits of a sizeable meal.

The behaviour of the Marsh Lions fits neatly with Packer's findings. Once the migration has headed back to the Serengeti, the lions often struggle to find enough food for their cubs and must hunt resident prey, such as warthogs, buffaloes and topis. Whenever there were only four

---

*At one time, the Paradise Pride comprised eight or more lionesses and three big males, and hunting buffaloes was a year-round occupation, though like all the lions if wildebeest were in their area they concentrated most of their efforts on hunting them. But they were so confident in their ability to deal with these fearsome prey animals that it was not uncommon to find them feasting on a buffalo even when wildebeest were available. Often they made it look easy, despite the fact that a full-grown bull can weigh 650kg (¾ ton) or more – twice the size of a zebra and almost three times heavier than a wildebeest. One or two of the Paradise lionesses were particularly adept at dealing with a buffalo. Sometimes they attacked the herd at night when it was more difficult for the buffaloes to defend their companions, and succeeded in killing a calf or a cow. But more often they focused their attention on the small groups of old bachelor males. In the middle of the day these were usually to be found chewing the cud at mud wallows out in the plains or lying up in ox-bows concealed among the riverine forest.*

*This was co-operative hunting at its most rewarding, as members of the pride rallied round to overpower a bull, surrounding it to ensure that there was always a lion ready to jump up onto his hindquarters whenever the bull swung round to defend his vulnerable rear end. The trick was to make sure that you didn't get tossed or killed. But there were times when the battle went on and on, and the buffalo eventually collapsed through exhaustion or from being eaten alive.*

*When drought strikes or a buffalo is sick and finds itself isolated, even a single lioness may attack and succeed in pulling it down, particularly if she is from a big pride and experienced in such matters. Despite a lioness's phenomenal strength, having knocked the buffalo over she now has a problem. This is when she must hope that other members of her pride – if she has them – will come to her assistance, and if they hear the buffalo's bellows of distress they certainly will do; if they don't she may well lose it to the hyenas. Alone she must attempt to prevent the buffalo from regaining its feet – and try to kill it. This may lead to a fierce wrestling match with the lioness using her weight and strength to pin the struggling animal to the ground, reaching across its back and straddling the buffalo's belly. Then she must edge forward so that she can bite into its throat, or better still clamp her jaws over its nose and mouth to suffocate it – the quickest way to kill a buffalo – which could still take up to ten minutes.*

The movements of the wildebeest migration are determined by the pattern of rainfall. Wildebeest prefer short green grass and move quickly to anywhere that it has rained and the grass will have burst into life.

lionesses in the pride they rarely attacked buffaloes, even though a large herd regularly moves through their territory and a number of bachelor herds containing old bulls are found in the area. Instead, the lions would focus their attentions on the warthogs, at times digging them out of their burrows as well as killing the occasional topi and scavenging from other predators whenever they could. Sometimes the lionesses would come upon a cow buffalo leading her young calf back to the herd, and in these circumstances might manage to chase the cow away and kill the calf. Once when this happened the cow wandered back searching for her calf, and even though the lionesses immediately reacted to the chance to attack her you could see the fear in their eyes as they circled, waiting for one of their companions to make the first move. Eventually one of the pride males came running over and grabbed the cow by the haunches. Only then did the lionesses gain sufficient confidence to close in and topple the cow onto her side. But when the number of adult lionesses in the Marsh Pride swelled to five or six they were far more likely to take buffaloes.

This was in marked contrast to the behaviour of the larger Paradise Pride, which lived to the south of Governor's Camp and whose territory enclosed the wide expanse of open plains between Rhino Ridge and the Mara River. The Paradise Pride were buffalo hunters through and through, regularly feasting on the kills that they made from the 500-strong herd that rotated around these lush pastures throughout the year. During the rains this area becomes waterlogged and difficult for a vehicle to navigate, as I have often found to my cost. But when tens of thousands of wildebeest darken the plains during the dry season it is a favourite spot for drivers to bring visitors eager to witness a river crossing. At times, dense throngs of wildebeest and zebras congregate along the riverbank, gathering at familiar crossing sites that the animals return to each year. And as often as not the Paradise Pride would be watching from the dense croton thickets bordering the river, ready to rush forward as the rest of the herd hurried to join those already in the water.

Hunting buffaloes may be the preserve of the larger groups of females and the best way for them to survive when easier prey isn't available, but they were still no better fed than a female foraging on her own. If lionesses hunting and foraging on their own got more food than individuals in small groups you would have expected small groups to break up when prey was scarce. But they didn't. In fact Packer and Scheel found that big groups broke down into smaller groups of four or five lionesses when prey was scarce and they were unable to find buffaloes to kill. In general, group size changed relatively infrequently, and did so more often when prey was abundant, but not because of the kind of prey the lions were hunting. The commonest reasons for these changes were when pride members gathered at a large kill; when they scattered during an encounter with males or females from another pride; when the mother of small cubs left to return to where she had hidden her cubs to suckle them; or when lions went off to drink, something they often do after eating.

The results proved to Packer that food alone was not enough to account for lionesses forming prides. In fact, far from lions being a solitary species whose members join forces to hunt, Packer feels that they should be thought of as a social species that occasionally has to split up to hunt most effectively, and sometimes assembles for a buffalo hunt if the pride is big enough. But if hunting wasn't the reason for lions remaining so loyal to their group, then what was? Packer and Pusey had already investigated the benefits of lionesses raising cubs in a crèche – it was one of their reasons for coming to the Serengeti and they watched nursing behaviour for well over 1,000 hours. They

had established that in the Serengeti the best scenario for rearing cubs successfully was for a group of two to five lionesses to rear cubs of a similar age communally, suckling them until they were weaned at around six to eight months, but maintaining the social environment of the crèche until the lionesses were ready to breed again, when their cubs were about a year and a half old. The females hunted together and returned to nurse their cubs together. Even when the cubs were weaned the crèche remained intact, with the cubs accompanying their mothers wherever they wandered.

By 'milking' some of the lionesses, Packer and Pusey found that a lioness's milk supply wasn't dependent on how many cubs were suckling from her, but on how well fed she was. This was the reason why a mother with a single cub could afford to allow other cubs to suckle from her. And the closer the relationship between the lionesses, the more likely they were to share their milk with each other's cubs. When the migration was in a pride's territory there was more than enough food for all the adults and large cubs, and

smaller cubs tended to do well too, as their mothers produced more milk after a large meal. This was the best time to watch lions, as the cubs were playful rather than listless, with the lionesses often joining in the fun.

But as most crèches are made up of from two to five lionesses, the lionesses are likely to be no better fed than if they were hunting on their own. And if they were hunting on their own and raising their cubs alone – as leopards and tigers do – the mother would probably get more to eat and the cubs would receive more milk than if they were part of a crèche. This is exactly what lionesses do for the first four to six weeks after giving birth, when they hide their cubs from predators and from the rest of the pride. But it is probably one of the few times that it makes sense for a lioness to isolate herself from her companions. Once the cubs are mobile it is safer to bring them to the pride and form a crèche. If there are no cubs of a similar age, a lioness can expect no help from her pride mates, and one might imagine that it would be to her advantage to try raising her cubs on her own. But Packer found that females in prides of up to seven adult lionesses were

All the lions are well fed when the migration is in their area, regardless of pride size; both cubs and adults are more playful during these times.

less vulnerable to male takeovers (and hence infanticide) than solitary females. It turns out that far from communal suckling being a benefit of group living for lions, it is the price that lionesses must pay for sticking together much of the time when their cubs are crèched. But the reason they do this is not just that it reduces the likelihood of infanticde.

A single lioness may be able feed herself, but without enough companions it is almost impossible for her to raise cubs – to do that you need a permanent place to live. The territory is a vital part of the jigsaw, though the pieces do not always fit neatly together. The boundaries of a pride's territories are somewhat fluid, and all prides move out at times, mostly in response to seasonal changes in prey availability. In addition, lionesses – either alone or in groups – quite often make long treks to where the wildebeest are congregating. Most prides have territories that overlap to some degree, though generally lions can avoid contact with non-pride mates by listening to roars and taking note of any scent left by other lions. Even so there is a real risk of meeting strangers and being attacked if you wander too far afield. We have often been surprised to find the Marsh Lions feeding on a kill well outside their territory, but usually when this happens most of the pride travel together in a defendable group. Fear of being isolated is one reason that the lions so often moved off together after they had fed; unless they were very hungry, none of them seemed to want to be the last to leave and risk being challenged without support if the territory holders suddenly appeared over the horizon.

During Packer and Scheel's study they found that on average prides encountered one another every four to five days, and in half these instances a chase took place, with the larger group winning on virtually every occasion. A quarter of encounters occurred at kills. If it was a big carcass, lionesses from the different prides sometimes fed together and only when most of the meat was eaten did they chase each other off. They behaved more like nomads, with each animal trying to eat as much as possible rather than wasting time fighting. Though food was sometimes contested it seemed as if the pride's primary goal was to defend their territory, and larger prides of up to ten lionesses were the most successful at doing this, raising more cubs and living longer.

No wonder, then, that small prides such as the Marsh Sisters – and members of crèches – rarely move around on their own. It is too dangerous to split up even if you might obtain more food. Lions' ability to go for long periods without eating – and then to feast – helps them to cope. If life becomes really difficult they can take a chance and hunt alone, or journey to where the migration is massed, and then hurry back to join their group. The fact that the bigger prides are rarely all together, and are often seen in intermediate group sizes of four or five individuals – either as a hunting group or as mothers forming a crèche – means that small prides have a greater chance of defending themselves in encounters with other territory holders. But groups of just one or two females are liable to lose their territories to larger neighbouring prides and must live a semi-nomadic life like Gimpy and Red. Solitary nomadic females might be well fed most of the time, but they are more vulnerable to attack from other groups of females and live shorter lives.

In the course of the last series of *Big Cat Diary* we had a graphic illustration of the dangers of a lioness moving around on her own, even when she is a member of a pride and stays in her territory. It involved one of the lionesses from the Ridge Pride, whose territory ranges from Rhino Ridge as far as Paradise Plain; over the last few years they have expanded into part of the Paradise Pride's territory, as the fortunes of that once powerful pride have waned. To the east lies the territory of the Topi Plains Pride, whose pride males once wreaked such havoc with Scar and the Marsh Pride and who are not averse to encroaching on the Ridge Pride's territory at times.

In the same way as the Bila Shaka lugga is the core area for the Marsh Pride, so the *Kichaka ya Nyoka* (place of the snake) is the heart of the Ridge Pride's territory. This lugga is flanked to the west by a rocky hill where the lions can still find a few dense patches of croton bushes as daytime resting places. The lugga and the croton thickets provide the favourite den sites for the Ridge Pride, and the previous year Angie and I had delighted in watching a crèche of four females and their young cubs in this area. At the time, three other Ridge Pride females were without cubs and from their behaviour it would have been easy to presume that they were from different prides. Both groups tended to go their separate ways when they wanted to hunt, and rarely did we find any of these other lionesses with the crèche, except perhaps when a member of the pride had made a large kill.

Angie and I had taken a particular interest in the two heavily maned Ridge Pride males, keeping track of their adventures since the days when they abandoned the Serena Pride and their half-grown cubs in the Mara Triangle and shifted their allegiance to a new pride of females. Early one morning four years ago the males had waded across the Mara River to take control of the Ridge Pride, and had since sired numerous cubs with their new partners. The males were in their prime when we first saw them, but by now they were visibly weary, and the dagger-like canines of the older male were worn-down stumps the colour of tobacco, while most of his incisors were missing. We were certain that the time had come for them to be driven out by younger, more vigorous males, yet here they still were having survived the annual influx of young nomads from the Serengeti. But the Topi Plains males seemed intent on claiming as much territory as they could and old males like this might well be forced to flee, just as Scar had done.

By the time we started filming, the 13 cubs in the crèche were about a year old, and mothers and cubs were still a tightly knit group. Meanwhile one of the other females had given birth along *Kichaka ya Nyoka*, though only one cub survived. We named him Solo and he became one of the stars of the series. Being so small Solo was easy for the audience to identify among the older cubs; he was the centre of attention for his older brothers and sisters and the focus of endless play sessions. To add some poignancy to his story, his mother was attacked and badly mauled by members of another pride, probably the Topi Plains females whom we occasionally found wandering as far west as *Kichaka ya Nyoka*.

One of the problems faced by Solo's mother was that the other members of the Ridge Pride, responding to the arrival of the migration, moved away from *Kichaka ya Nyoka* when the little cub was about eight weeks old. Now that Solo had started to eat meat, he would have to compete with the older cubs if his mother decided to rejoin the pride. Perhaps that was why she doggedly remained at *Kichaka ya Nyoka*. On her own she could still find plenty to eat for herself and Solo, and on more than one occasion we found her with a freshly killed wildebeest or watched as she stalked along the bottom of the lugga unseen by the herds until she exploded from right under their noses where they had gathered to drink. But there was always the danger that she might bump into other lions with no one to help her, and sure enough she eventually did.

When I first saw Solo's mother after the attack I didn't even recognize her; she was so battered and looked so old, she could hardly stand, let alone walk, as she limped her way up and over Rhino Ridge. By the evening she had managed to reach some shade and had linked up with one of the pride males. At one point he came over and licked her, then lay down a few metres away. She would be safer here, among the pride. Her hindquarters were a mass of cuts and bites, her tail torn and ripped – wounds typical of what happens when a group of lionesses corners a lone female and is able to really beat her up. Over the years I have seen a number of lions with only half a tail, or the tail-tip missing, due to vicious scraps with other lions. The aggressors use the same strategy as when attacking a buffalo, encircling their victim, being careful to avoid its dangerous front end. As one or more lions menace their opponent from the front, snarling and

Solo of the Ridge Pride at three months. As the only small cub in the pride, he became the object of intense interest – and fun and games – for his older brothers and sisters.

Solo was one of the stars of the last series of *Big Cat Diary*. Young cubs always guarantee plenty of social activity in the pride, to the delight of film crews and visitors.

lunging head to head, others close in from behind, slicing through skin and flesh with their claws, trying to bite into their opponent's spine. Every time the lioness spins round to face her tormentors she is attacked again and again at her most vulnerable point – her rear end. Which is why it is such a huge advantage in these circumstances to have companions. Even one extra ally may allow you to break free of the stranglehold a group can exert on a single opponent.

How Solo's mother escaped with her life I do not know. But lions have a remarkable ability to heal themselves, licking their wounds to keep them clean, and because she was a member of a pride rather than a nomad she could rely on feeding from kills made by other pride members, giving her the chance to recover. However, there was no sign of Solo and we all feared that the inevitable had happened: either the Topi Plains males or their females had killed the cub. But much to our relief, we found him later that afternoon, tucked in among the

croton bushes, not far from where the male and his mother rested.

Just as we were about to finish filming the third series, Solo disappeared again. We found his mother over towards *Kichaka ya Nyoka*, calling with that soft call that lionesses use – an intimate 'come hither' sound meant for little ears, not the resounding roar with which lions communicate at a distance. We had seen lionesses call like this before after losing a cub in a fracas of some sort. Something must have happened during the night quite close to where Solo's mother was now calling, though at least on this occasion she showed no sign of injuries. Perhaps the Topi Plains males really had found Solo and killed him.

Solo's mother was clearly distressed, salivating profusely, reluctant to abandon the search. It was late in the morning for her to be wandering around, and she was clearly hot and tired. Back and forth she went, before finally turning and heading over Rhino Ridge, towards the place where

the other members of the pride were resting. Every so often she stopped and roared, then listened. But there was no response. We followed, thoroughly depressed at this sudden turn of events. We always knew that it would be difficult for Solo's mother to raise a solitary cub in these circumstances. The migration had begun its annual exodus back to the Serengeti. A small cub will always struggle to get a fair share of food at a kill when times are tough, and may well starve. Little wonder then that a lioness sometimes abandons a single cub. Hard as it seems, it is probably the best strategy for a mother. Better to start again and produce another, larger litter, and form part of a crèche if she can, than battle to raise a single cub for too long and then fail. Whether you raise one or four cubs, it will still take you a year and a half of your life to do it.

But this story had a happy ending. We found Solo later that morning. Earlier on he had been seen feeding at a wildebeest kill, with one of the other lionesses and her large cub. He then separated from the other two and took refuge among the long grass in a lugga. He looked distressed and dehydrated by the time we found him, and every so often emerged from his hiding place and moved around as if not sure what to do. I couldn't help wondering if he might have settled down more easily and felt more secure if he had litter mates. Eventually he retreated to the lugga again and did what was best – waited for his mother to find him. Occasionally a cub gets left behind and the mother never returns to claim it, though generally not when a cub is as fit and healthy as Solo. I was wondering how I was going to explain to the *Big Cat Diary* viewers that Solo had disappeared. Having spent the past ten weeks watching his development I had begun to feel responsible for his safety, though I knew that there was nothing we could do to intervene.

*Big Cat Diary* might appear to be a soap opera, but for the cats it's real life – and at times an untimely death. We can't change the script. Fortunately, later that evening Solo's mother wandered down the rise from her resting place under a large fig tree at the top of Rhino Ridge. Was she attracted to the sight of our vehicles, knowing that the presence of cars sometimes points to where other lions are gathered? Maybe she could pick up Solo's scent, or the scent of other members of her pride. She had already walked this way earlier in the day, and then to our dismay stopped short, preferring the shade of the tree. Perhaps she knew Solo was here somewhere and no longer felt the urgency to find him during the heat of the day, when most lions would be resting under cover. Lions live by a different sense of time to humans. We all raised a silent cheer as the little cub responded to his mother's softly uttered contact call and ran to meet her. He pushed his head up under her chin in greeting before settling down to suckle. It was as if nothing had happened.

Solo at two months, relaxing with his mother. Lionesses vary considerably in their mothering ability, though over time individual lionesses in a pride generally have similar success in breeding.

# The Bonds of Kinship

Those animals that help each other most are usually close relatives, and the idea of kin selection has been widely acknowledged in the animal kingdom to explain altruism or 'helping' behaviour. This certainly appears to be the case with lions, although they achieve their goals in life in rather different ways to most other mammalian predators. Take spotted hyenas, for instance. Females are heavier than males and are the dominant sex in a clan, with cubs born to dominant females being destined for high status. They are often better fed than other youngsters, because their mother uses her size and rank to assert herself at kills, and they take precedence at carcasses over any hyena of lower rank. But despite the presence of a dominance hierarchy, all the females in a spotted hyena clan breed.

A wild dog pack is organized somewhat differently, with males being slightly larger than females. As with hyenas, both sexes are organized into separate dominance hierarchies, but with the dogs neither sex is dominant. The top male and female form the dominant or alpha pair and these two monopolize breeding in the pack, with the dominant female giving birth to an average of ten pups per litter annually (a single litter of 19 puppies has been recorded). The other adults forsake their own chance to breed – unless they emigrate and try to form a new pack – and help the dominant pair raise the pups; this makes genetic sense only because all the 'helpers' are related to the puppies. Adult males usually outnumber females by at least two to one, due to the fact that sisters and daughters of the alpha female must emigrate if they want to breed – daughters always do, thereby helping to prevent inbreeding within a pack.

Lionesses don't form dominance hierarchies that restrict breeding rights to just a few individuals. By analysing many years of breeding records from 560 females in 31 prides living in the Ngorongoro Crater and the Serengeti, Craig Packer and his co-

Mutual grooming removes ticks from parts of a lion's coat that they are unable to reach themselves, and helps to maintain bonds among pride members.

Khali (right) and her two-year-old daughter being greeted by two of
Khali's next litter of cubs, aged twelve weeks.

workers were able to track every cub that
reached its first birthday and identify its
mother. They found that all the lionesses in
a pride had roughly equal success in raising
cubs. There were certain years, of course,
when some did better than others, but over
time it evened itself out with all the
lionesses having the opportunity to breed.
As Packer reported, 'The major finding is
that the females in the lion pride really
form a true community where there's no
bosses and everybody's much the same.' It
would be hard for these powerful animals
to enforce a hierarchy, as individuals are all
too capable of defending themselves and
fighting back when necessary. Also, any
lioness who tried to prevent a relative from
mating would risk the wrath of her male
partner, who would no doubt drive the
interfering female away. Constant
harassment and fighting would not be in
the group's interest.

But even though lionesses are
democratic when it comes to reproduction,
and co-operate in raising their young, they
aren't quite the paragons of virtue that
people once thought. Not all lionesses are
brave-hearted in defence of their territory,
nor do individuals always pull their weight
when it comes to hunting. In fact it seems
that, rather like humans, lions at times
cheat on their pride mates, doing as little as
they can and relying on others to provide
the food or take the lead in repelling
intruders.

Over the years people have speculated
on the degree to which lions co-operate
when hunting. One myth long since
dispelled scripted a leading role for the
male lion in the proceedings. In this
scenario the male would suddenly reveal
himself at just the right moment to a group
of wildebeest or zebras – perhaps even roar
– as part of a well-orchestrated game plan
to stampede prey into the path of the
hidden lionesses. But more often than not
when a male lion with a mane as big as a
haystack walks out onto centre stage he's
the last thing the lionesses want to see,
unless they are hunting a buffalo. Instead
the lionesses are left looking perplexed as
to why the object of their hunt has
suddenly bolted. Of course it is of little
consequence to the male if he is less than
cautious in such circumstances; he can
pretty much do what he wants, even if it
means ruining a hunt. The females will kill
sooner or later anyway, and when they do
he is assured of getting something to eat.

So how much do the lionesses really co-
operate in trying to catch their prey? When
a herd of wildebeest comes galloping
towards a group intent on hunting, it often
appears as if each female is simply trying to
get as close as possible to the prey and
catch it for herself. Co-operation seems to
be limited to watching what the other
hunters are doing and adjusting your
position relative to them to maximize your
chance of catching the prey, though simply
by fanning out the lionesses could be said
to be co-operating and increasing the
chance of capturing one or more
wildebeest. And sometimes a lioness holds
her position as if expecting one of her pride

*Though all members of a pride 'cheat' at times, letting their pride mates hunt for them, there is no doubt that certain individuals stand out within the group, expert at tackling particular species of prey or just quicker or more experienced, more wily. They are quite often the first to attempt to stalk prey when a hunting opportunity presents itself, though this can also depend on how hungry an individual is. Loony, as we nicknamed her, was one such animal among the Marsh Pride. She just loved to hunt, and was amazingly proficient at it. When Loony was hunting, other members of the pride could afford to watch rather than participate, taking advantage of their pride mate's prowess.*

*We filmed Loony more than 20 years ago for a BBC-TV Wildlife on One programme called 'Ambush at Masai Mara'. The book of The Marsh Lions, which I had co-authored with my friend Brian Jackman, was about to be published and the programme followed the story of the pride over a three-week period during the migration. Brian and I camped with wildlife film-maker Hugh Miles among the riverine forest at the edge of Musiara Marsh. Loony became the star of that film and entertained and enthralled us with her hunting ability, setting our adrenaline pulsing at the sight of her sleek body accelerating through the long dry grass as she closed with her prey. I can still remember the last night of filming, with Loony tackling yet another wildebeest as it crossed the Bila Shaka lugga, heading for Paradise Plain and the river-crossing sites. The light had almost gone as Loony saw her chance, and in no time she was hanging upside down, lion and wildebeest locked together in a deadly embrace. Loony's powerful forearms encircled her victim's neck, her vice-like jaws suffocating it, as she braced herself by digging her hind claws into its flesh. It was one of the most memorable scenes I have witnessed. Not a sound was uttered as the darkness closed in, life ebbing away from one animal, providing food for another.*

mates to make a move and perhaps enable her to ambush a fleeing animal more easily.

Equally, it is very apparent when watching a hunt that there are times when an individual chooses to let a pride mate take the initiative rather than joining her in the hunt, thus conserving energy and avoiding the risk of injury – cheating, in fact. If the hunter is successful, the watcher knows that unless it is a very small kill, pride membership entitles her to a share of the spoils. Scientists with the Serengeti Lion Project found that lions are least likely to help one another in situations where their pride mates are likely to be successful hunting on their own, such as when a warthog or wildebeest is the object of the stalk. But if more powerful prey such as a zebra or buffalo is the target, then a helping hand will probably increase the chance of a successful hunt, and it is in these circumstances that lions are most likely to help. Zebras, particularly the stallions, are hefty creatures who can kick with the ferocity of a mustang and bite through a man's arm. They will lash out with their sharp hooves when a lioness tries to grab them by the rump, occasionally leaving her with a broken jaw and the prospect of a

lingering death. But if two lionesses co-operate in chasing the zebra, they have a better chance of overpowering it and pulling it to the ground, however vigorously it tries to defend itself. A kill like this will provide them with food for two or three days – if there aren't too many hyenas around for them to fend off.

Certainly one would expect older females to be more adept than their younger relatives when it comes to hunting, even though all cats from the earliest age

Lions have very expressive faces, with the black lips helping to frame the powerful teeth. This lioness is baring her teeth in a defensive threat, telling any cubs to stop pestering her or warning another adult not to approach.

A five-to-six-month-old-cub from the Ridge Pride practises a killing bite on a topi carcass. Lions have a long period of dependence and even at two years of age may be clumsy, inexperienced killers.

have the innate ability to stalk, crouch, pounce and bite. By accompanying the adults, young lions gradually learn what to hunt, after numerous adventures chasing elephants and hippos or mongooses and civets. They also gain experience in how best to overpower different kinds of prey and in refining the killing bite to throat or muzzle, something that it takes time for them to master. Young females have the luxury of honing their hunting skills within the security of the pride, unless they are forced out as subadults. And young males who leave their natal pride at the time of a takeover are fortunate if their sisters or female cousins are evicted with them, as they will benefit from the lionesses' superior hunting ability for as long as they stay together.

I have often wondered if solitary lionesses aren't forced to develop their hunting skills to new heights simply to survive; they certainly don't have the luxury of cheating. Large groups may at times end up at a disadvantage because their companions refuse to co-operate in capturing prey. But lions adapt their needs according to circumstances, and prides may adopt different strategies according to the

strengths and abilities of individual pride members and the requirements of hunting particular prey. In Etosha National Park in Namibia, where springboks are an important but flighty prey for lions to capture, prides co-operate to a greater degree than is generally seen in the Serengeti. The flat open terrain of this

semi-arid region favours the springbok, and only by working together can lions have any chance of capturing these fleet-footed antelopes. Lionesses fan out into favoured positions, some moving in a wide arc to outflank their prey, while others wait for the rest to rush forward, grabbing the springboks as they attempt to flee. A hunt is most successful when all the lionesses have time to take up their positions.

With relatedness being so crucial to current ideas of what has shaped lion society, it came as a surprise when the findings of a study by a young American couple, Mark and Delia Owens, seemed to contradict this assumption. Their observations on lions in the Central Kalahari Game Reserve in Botswana painted a very different portrait of life among the pride from the one that had become so familiar from the Serengeti. The biggest surprise was that the Kalahari lionesses they were studying seemed to switch prides – and pride areas – frequently during the dry season. In their book *Cry of the Kalahari* the Owenses say:

Despite their long canines, lions often fail to penetrate a wildebeest's 1cm (½in) thick skin, with death being caused by strangulation rather than haemorrhage.

*Without exception, all the lionesses we monitored associated with members of different prides. The cohesion and pride structure that was so permanent and fundamental to the social organization of Serengeti lions had temporarily disintegrated in the Kalahari population. It was a startling example of how a species can adjust its social system to extreme environments.*

*We could no longer be certain that the females of a pride were related: it was impossible to know the family origins of the older ones, whom we had not observed from birth. We had always assumed that Chary, the oldest, had grown up in the Blue Pride, but she may have been born and raised in the East Side Pride. And we could not ascertain the paternity of cubs born under these conditions, for the females of the Blue Pride mated with males from four different prides.*

During the rains, the Kalahari lions acted like most other lions, tenaciously clinging to territories staked out where prey was most abundant. But when the dry season set in they dispersed widely, roaming huge areas as a way of coping with the region's sparse and unpredictable food supply. They were able to survive indefinitely without water, conserving moisture by adopting a nocturnal existence and drinking the blood and body fluids of their prey.

The Kalahari lions' more nomadic lifestyle is comparable to the way wild dogs on the Serengeti plains cope with scattered and far-ranging prey. They are forced to cover huge areas – up to 2,000km² (800sq. miles) – due to the migratory lifestyle of their main prey species in this region, the wandering herds of Thomson's gazelles and wildebeest. For many years the Serengeti plains were considered prime wild dog habitat, partly because the dogs were so visible out on the plains and drew the attention of numerous film crews. But as people began to study wild dogs in woodland habitats and bush country, such as in Kruger in South Africa, where there is an abundance of resident prey such as impalas and kudus, they found that the dogs needed home ranges of only 500–800km² (200–320sq. miles) – less than half the size required by the Serengeti plains packs. The manner in which food supply can affect an animal's behaviour was apparent in other ways, too. Normally, as we have seen, only the dominant female in each wild dog pack breeds. If a second female gives birth, the dominant female generally tries to take control of the puppies or may kill them, particularly if food is at a premium. But in the woodlands, where prey is plentiful, more than one female sometimes manages to breed without antagonism. A degree of flexibility in the behavioural repertoire of a species has survival value for the population and the individual, allowing both to maximize breeding opportunities when better conditions prevail. Wild dog puppies are able to follow their adult relatives once they are three months old, allowing the pack to return to its nomadic lifestyle. But for a lion, raising cubs while wandering over such huge distances just doesn't work.

The Owenses found that the nine females of the Blue Pride – their local pride – increased their range by 450 per cent, from 700km² (280sq. miles) in the wet

By hunting in a pack wild dogs are able to kill animals as large as full-grown wildebeest, which weigh up to 270kg (595lb), compared to a dog's 20–25kg (44–55lb).

Elephants are a huge force for change in any environment, opening up woodlands and changing the balance of woodland and grassland over time.

season to over 3,885km² (1550sq. miles) in the dry months; the Springbok Pan Pride increased their pride area by 650 per cent. Lions on the Serengeti plains, where the majority live a nomadic existence, face similar problems in trying to find sufficient food all year round and to form prides. The Kalahari lions often looked thin during the lengthy dry season; there was rarely enough food to allow the lionesses to stay together in large prides and it was pointless for them to attempt to defend a territory of thousands of square kilometres. Under such difficult circumstances cub survival was minimal. In parts of the Kalahari lion densities are ten times lower than in Serengeti and Kruger. Rainfall is the key here. Where rainfall is better distributed, as in the Mara and parts of the Serengeti, prey is much more readily available year round and lions can afford a well-developed loyalty to place.

More recently, Paul Funston has made a study of Kalahari lions in the newly

proclaimed Kgalagadi Transfrontier Park, a vast area of semi-desert dune country interspersed by vegetated dune valleys and dry riverbeds which includes territory in Botswana, Namibia and South Africa. Funston found that lions living in the dune country often formed large prides, but spent much of the time as dynamic subgroups. When they could find them, these smaller groups hunted oryx, an animal large enough to provide them with food for several days. Otherwise, they subsisted on smaller animals such as steenboks, spring hares, porcupines and aardvarks. Perhaps part of what the Owenses had witnessed in the Central Kalahari, when 'non-relatives' joined up to form prides, were in fact subgroups that had spent time away from their pride and then joined up again when better conditions prevailed or when their cubs had become independent. Though lions in the Serengeti–Mara seem very reluctant to rejoin relatives if separated for too long, it

is quite possible that this could happen in more extreme environments such as the Kalahari, where such divisions occur regularly and none of the lions are able to stay in large groups in a restricted territory all year round. Preferable by far to rejoin relatives if you can rather than forge relationships with non-relatives.

One thing that is undisputed is that due to the harshness of these semi-desert environments, it is harder for females to raise cubs. Starvation is a potent cause of death among most lion populations; in the Serengeti it accounts for 25 per cent of cub deaths. In the Kalahari it is not unusual for none of a litter to survive or for a female to be forced to abandon her cubs during the dry season. Life for subadults is almost as tough – Funston found that up to 70 per cent of subadult males died after being forced from their pride, mainly from starvation. Branching out on your own, when still relatively inexperienced, is always going to be tough, but at least in the

Serengeti and Kruger these young males can often survive by ganging together to hunt large animals such as buffaloes. But buffaloes are particularly sensitive to drought, so they do not occur in the Kalahari. Often young male lions wander outside the park in a desperate search for food, come into conflict with ranchers and are shot. During the Owenses' study more than 30 per cent of all the lions they tagged or collared were shot by professional hunters, poachers or ranchers.Young lionesses seem more adept at surviving than males – they can target small prey more easily and often linger for as long as possible in the territory of their birth.

During favourable times for cubs to be born, Funston discovered that litters contained twice as many males as females, presumably a way of compensating for the higher mortality among subadult males: normally the sex ratio at birth is 1:1. Funston witnessed first-hand just how difficult life can be for the lions. For several weeks he tracked one lioness with seven large cubs (some of whom belonged to two relatives who had been shot). It became a desperate struggle for survival after the lioness tore ligaments in her hind leg trying to tackle a large oryx on her own. Unable to hunt, the group barely ate for six weeks. At one point the lioness managed to join up with three younger relatives with small cubs, and through her persistence overcame their initial aggression. But the competition for food between two groups with different aged cubs meant that the arrangement just couldn't work, and the younger lionesses moved away to try to ensure that their three small cubs survived. The lone lioness and older cubs eventually died of starvation.

As Funston points out, one of the benefits of subgroups is that 'if a subgroup is shot when it ventures out of the park, only part of a pride is lost'. He also discovered that the lion population of the Kgalagadi Transfrontier Park was larger than had been thought, with 450 lions in 18

prides, a population not dissimilar in size to that of the Masai Mara, except that the Mara is 1,510km² (600sq. miles) while the Kgalagadi is 36,000km² (14,000sq. miles). Though a number of lions are killed each year by trophy hunters and livestock owners, Funston feels that the population is large enough to sustain the current offtake.

Just how much flexibility exists in lion behaviour has been witnessed by a novel translocation experiment conducted at Phinda Resource Reserve in South Africa.

With suitable lion habitat shrinking at an alarming rate, it is encouraging to find that in some parts of Africa attempts are being made to reclaim farmland and restock it with wild animals. There is little doubt that in many cases wildlife is the best form of land use, particularly in marginal areas where the quest for short-term gain often leads to habitat degradation and the impoverishment of the local people. Wildlife is generally far better adapted to cycles of drought and deluge than cattle or

By the early 20th Century the southern population of white rhinos was virtually wiped out, with just a few hundred surviving in South Africa. Through the work of dedicated conservationists they now number 11,000.

cash crops. In addition to this, wildlife-based tourism has huge potential in many parts of Africa and is the reason why many farmers abandon cattle-ranching and agriculture for the money that wildlife can earn them.

Phinda is a privately owned sanctuary of 180km² (70sq. miles) some 300km (200 miles) north of Durban on the Maputaland coastal plain. Not so long ago this used to be ranching country, where cattle and barbed wire fences were the norm. Today these have been replaced by thousands of wildebeest, zebras, giraffes and other ungulates. There are elephants and white rhinos too – everything that lived here in pre-colonial times, including lions, leopards and cheetahs. As little as 50 years ago big cats thrived here, before cattle ranchers and farmers wiped them out.

When it was decided to reintroduce large predators to Phinda, landowners bordering the reserve were naturally concerned about suddenly finding lions on their doorsteps. Similar projects elsewhere in Africa had not met with great success, and many big cats were shot when they moved out onto private land. To try to prevent the same thing happening at Phinda, the lions and cheetahs due for release were radio-collared to make sure that the staff always knew where they were and could report back to the local communities. Luke Hunter, a young Australian zoologist, was given the job of co-ordinating the reintroduction programme and monitoring the cats' movements.

Most cats become very attached to their home range, and may have lived there all their lives. It is hardly surprising, then, that when a stock-raiding leopard, for instance, is translocated, the first thing it does is to try to make its way home, even if this involves a journey of many kilometres. In the past, big cats were generally released the moment they arrived at their new location – a procedure known as 'hard release'. Not unexpectedly, they either headed straight back to their old range or were never seen again. With this in mind, Phinda tried a different approach, allowing their lions to settle down in a larger enclosure for a period of about eight weeks. Here they were able to absorb the sense of place, the sounds and sights of the neighbourhood, the ambience that is unique to any area. This 'soft release' approach had never been tried before with big cats, but it worked.

Settling the lions in was only one of the problems that Hunter and his team had to face. Most lions available for reintroduction are single animals or small groups that have left protected areas and need to be removed. Consequently, Phinda didn't have a ready-made pride of lions to release into the reserve. Instead they had to build a pride of their own as lions became available. This meant breaking all the rules of lion society and mixing relatives and non-relatives together. But introducing individuals to one another gradually allowed them to become conditioned to strangers and build the bonds necessary for pride life, just as sometimes happens when nomadic male lions gradually build up an association with non-relatives at a kill or elsewhere on their wanderings and end up forming a coalition for life.

Much to Hunter's relief and delight, when the first 13 lions were released the adult lionesses maintained their homemade alliances with non-relatives and behaved as if they had been born and raised together, suckling each other's cubs and helping to defend their territory against other lions. The lions quickly staked out territories of about 100km² (40sq. miles), comparable to an average-sized lion territory in similar habitat elsewhere in southern Africa. The sudden emergence of large predators initially caught Phinda's prey species by

Two of the Marsh lionesses play-fighting. Lionesses will fight to defend their territory against other groups of lionesses.

Khali gently deterring one of her cubs from trying to suckle. A lioness with a small litter is more likely to let other cubs suckle from her.

surprise, with the result that the lions found hunting easy and were able to make multiple kills. But by the end of the first year the prey animals had increased the time spent on vigilance by about 200 per cent, and a more normal predator-prey relationship was established.

One of the biggest challenges facing the reintroduction programme was the acute shortage of adult male lions available for translocation. All the introduced males were just 18–24 months old, barely old enough under normal circumstances to leave their pride. Though male lions may be sexually mature and capable of producing sperm at 26 months, they do not normally get the opportunity to breed until they are four or five years old, wandering as nomads until they are big enough to challenge established territory holders. Males as young as the Phinda ones would have no chance of defending themselves in a dispute with groups of full-grown males. They would be attacked and chased away. But as the Phinda programme demonstrated, it is behaviour rather than physiology that determines when they breed.

It isn't only the adult males who keep young males from staying on in their natal pride. Adult lionesses are usually particularly intolerant of young males – even though they may be their sons or nephews – once they have a new litter of cubs to provide for; apart from anything else, finding food for the new generation is now the priority. But when the first lions were released at Phinda there were no adult males, and the lionesses did not have cubs. So at the age of 21 months the young Phinda males became the consorts of the adult lionesses and a few months later when they started to produce sperm their efforts to impregnate the females bore fruit. They acted just like full-grown males, soon started to dominate the females at kills and did little hunting for themselves.

Many species exhibit this kind of precocial behaviour, as it is known, when a new environment opens up to them. It is nature's way of filling a vacuum, allowing a species to breed up rapidly to the carrying capacity of the land. When rinderpest (a viral form of bovine measles) was eradicated from the cattle population surrounding the Serengeti–Mara by the veterinary services in the 1950s, it allowed the wildebeest population to explode from

200,000 animals in the 1960s to over one million by the late 1970s. Young female wildebeest, who normally have their first calf in their third year, started breeding in their second year. Nature has a remarkable ability to repopulate an area if left to its own devices.

Luke Hunter watched as these bands of young male lions aggressively staked out territories or tried to expand existing ones in their quest for breeding rights with the lionesses. They scent-marked and roared; they patrolled their territories and fought when they had to over turf. One coalition of young males, who were less than three years old at the time, even indulged in infanticide when they took over a new territory, killing the first two litters of cubs born at Phinda. But the losses were balanced by the lionesses' ability to breed again quickly, and the fact that lionesses at Phinda started mating at two years of age and conceived at 32 months, far younger than normal. With an abundance of prey,

plenty of space and low levels of competition, the lions enjoyed ideal conditions for population growth in those early days, and the race to breed was at its peak. This is life at its least stressful for lions, and all these factors no doubt combined to make the reintroduction such a success in its critical early stages.

Humans were the biggest problem. Five lions and two cheetahs were killed in wire snares at Phinda within the first five years of their release. The loss of pride males for whatever reason creates the opportunity for pride takeovers, and five cubs were lost to infanticide as a result of snaring. By 1999 at least ten attempts had been made to re-establish lion populations in areas of South Africa where they had been eradicated, ranging from national parks to co-operative reserves comprising private owners and rural communities. Part of their success has hinged on the inclusion of anti-poaching measures and outreach programmes to sensitize the local communities to wildlife conservation. Only if local communities share in the benefits of conservation will they be effective in the long term.

Encouraging as these efforts are in helping to ensure a future for Africa's big cats, small areas such as Phinda, and Nakuru or Nairobi National Parks in Kenya, face problems inherent in their size. Though they are far more than large zoos, their smallness can prompt an escalation in aggression among their feline residents and increased emigration. And when epidemic diseases strike they can decimate a small population. Phinda may yet solve the problem of lack of space by an initiative supported by government, private landowners and local communities who have earmarked a total of 3,000km² (1,200sq. miles) – an area twice the size of the Masai Mara – to form one contiguous park. More space would mean that the number of cats could be increased, helping to solve another of the problems facing isolated populations – inbreeding and all its repercussions: higher than average

Khali's two-year-old daughter spent a lot of time with her younger siblings – we often found them playing together early in the morning.

Small cubs are full of nonsense – and full of confidence when their larger pride mates are around. With such impressive protectors to hand, the youngsters can afford to play and frolic.

valuable lessons to be learned from this as it becomes increasingly necessary to manage wildlife areas and regulate numbers artificially.

Butch Smuts wrote a fascinating book called *Lion*, describing his work in Kruger during the 1970s. Smuts was one of the first people to use the call-in technique for counting lions, setting up recording stations at strategic points and playing the sounds of hyenas on a kill. He had studied zebra ecology before beginning his work on lions, at a time when oscillations in the numbers of wildebeest and zebras were giving cause for concern. Both species were at high levels after a number of dry years and were culled in an effort to reduce overgrazing. The cycle reversed in the 1970s when rainfall was above average, allowing the dominant grazer the buffalo to increase dramatically, with wildebeest and zebra numbers falling. Even though culling was discontinued in 1974, wildebeest and zebra populations continued to decline and it was realized that other factors were involved – in particular lions. Smuts was able to show that areas with the greatest number of lions also had the highest rate of mortality among zebra foals, and that lions were important in regulating the zebra and wildebeest populations. In an attempt to reduce predation on these two species and to protect tsessebes and sables, both rare in Kruger, 335 lions were culled from three areas of Kruger's Central District.

Unfortunately, due to foot and mouth restrictions, it wasn't possible to translocate any of the lions. Even when the disease was eradicated, lions still had to be culled. By examining the carcasses it was possible to deduce what species the lions had been preying on: a preponderance of impala, followed by wildebeest, giraffe, zebra and then warthog. The question now was whether the lions would continue to suppress wildebeest and zebra numbers or turn to other prey. At the time lions were still targeting wildebeest even when they were in low numbers.

infertility and poorer than average immunity, increasing the risk that an epidemic disease could endanger the entire population. As Luke Hunter says, 'Some critics see this brand of active management as unwarranted interference. But in a world where wildlife populations are becoming smaller and increasingly fragmented, we are rarely afforded the luxury of "letting nature take its course". Planning, manipulation and management were essential parts of

the Phinda programme. Together they hold out new hope for the big cats and perhaps represent the future of conservation in Africa.'

Even protected areas the size of Kruger – a massive wedge of wild bushveld even larger than the Serengeti – which harbours one of the largest lion populations in Africa, have struggled over the years in their attempts to find a balance between predators and their prey, though there are

The Topi Plains Pride at play. Large prides are more successful at defending their territory and at raising cubs, with lionesses in big prides living longer than solitary females.

This finding echoed elements of Judith Rudnai's study of the Nairobi Park lions, which had been prompted partly by concerns about the impact the lions were having on the wildebeest population. Wildebeest numbers had plummeted in the wake of the devastating drought of 1960, yet the lions still targeted the wildebeest in preference to other prey and there were fears that the herds might be wiped out. So it was a relief for the park's management when the lions switched their attentions to the Coke's hartebeest, and though they still favoured wildebeest this species began to form a less disproportionate part of their diet. In fact, wildebeest numbers increased during the time of Rudnai's study.

More recently, as the human population has exploded around Nairobi Park, illegal meat hunting has become a way of life for some of the people. The number of wildebeest and zebras migrating into the park during the dry season from the southern plains has fallen dramatically, forcing some of the lions to move out in their search for food and leading inevitably to conflict with livestock owners. As a result, the lion population has almost halved and the voices of those who want to

see the Kitengela corridor fenced off to keep the animals in the park – and the people out – is getting louder by the day.

In Kruger, much to Smuts' surprise, the lion population had almost returned to previous levels 17 months later, though some of the groups were still unsettled, paying little attention to territorial boundaries and travelling widely, similar in many ways to nomadic lions. Sometimes members of unrelated groups fed on baits, and after some initial squabbling settled down to feed as if they were from the same pride; in two instances subadult lions originating from different prides even formed a single new group. This seemed the best option for the young lions if they were to succeed in staking out a territory, rather than remaining in smaller groups (or on their own) as nomads. The absence of roaring, scent marks and the physical presence of lions quickly made it apparent if an area was safe for newcomers to enter. Smuts concluded that removing a large number of prides from one area led to an influx of outsiders from further afield, causing greater disruption and a reduction in breeding success. A better solution was to cull more selectively. When only a few

individuals are lost from neighbouring prides or when only one pride is removed at a time, less conspicuous vacancies are created. This results in a lower incursion of new lions, or only a single group entering a vacant area. Often these turn out to be stable groups from a neighbouring pride, which simply extend their range, and reproduction seems to be more successful.

Subadults, particularly males, are drawn to a vacuum created by culling, trophy-

hunting or disease. This is to be expected, as the subadults are the nucleus of new prides and are always on the look-out for unoccupied areas in which to establish themselves. The ability of lions to recolonize an area quickly is due in part to their short gestation period, and in part to the fact that where lions have been artificially removed cub survival is enhanced due to less competition. Lions who have been persecuted become far more shy and wary, lying up in cover during the hours of daylight and moving around only after dark.

In hindsight, Smuts felt that the culling experiment had not been a success in its main aim, which was to reduce predation on specific prey species. More extensive culling would have been necessary to reduce the lion population significantly. He would far rather have let nature take its course and allow predators and prey to stabilize on their own, echoing sentiments expressed 70 years earlier by the first warden of the Kruger, James Stevenson-Hamilton. But as the decline in wildebeest and zebra numbers had been exacerbated by previous culls, more powerful voices felt it only right that man should now try to lend a helping hand.

Unlike wildebeest, zebras live in family units consisting of a stallion and up to five or six mares and their foals. These family groups retain their identity when migrating in large herds.

# At the Hand of Man

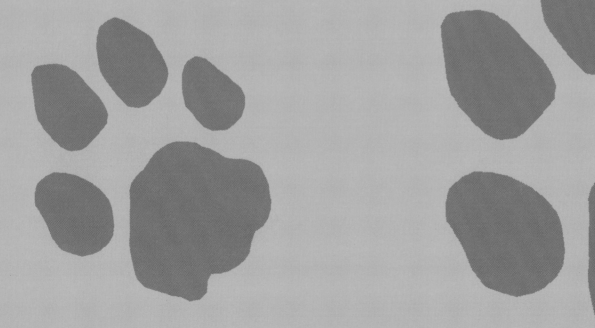

Contrary to the concerns of the first park wardens, predators have proved to be the best game managers, helping to keep prey populations healthy by weeding out the sick and the old, and dampening the effect of severe fluctuations in numbers that might otherwise damage the environment. Despite this fact, the greatest threat to lions is still man. In the last 50 years the world's human population has more than doubled to nearly six billion. By 2025 it is estimated to reach 8.5 billion, stabilizing at around 11.6 billion in 2200 – or about 90 people per km² (230 per sq. mile). In our overpopulated world, there is little room for wild lions.

The ever-increasing demand for land to grow crops and ranch livestock is destroying the last remnants of wilderness. Stands of ancient hardwoods in Indonesia's national

A lioness is fiercely protective of her cubs and will charge a man on foot when disturbed.

The Marsh Pride feeding on a wildebeest at the edge of Musiara Marsh,
close to where the Big Cat Diary camp is hidden among the riverine forest.

parks are felled to cater for the demand for exotic hardwoods in Europe and North America, leaving one of our closest relatives, the orang-utan, with nowhere to live. The American government, far from providing a lead to the rest of the world, refuses to sign the Kyoto accord to help protect our environment and proposes instead to drill for oil in the Arctic wildlife reserve, home of one of the last great animal migrations, more than 130,000 caribou. How is the developed world – which consumes the bulk of the world's natural resources – going to play an effective role in helping the poorer nations preserve their wildlife heritage when it is so indebted to big business and guided by a warped sense of self-interest?

Ever since 1872, when President Ulysses S. Grant signed the bill creating Yellowstone – the world's first national park – conservationists have been forced endlessly to reinvent themselves in an attempt to salvage a fragment of our past. Many of Africa's parks and reserves were created during colonial times. If land was considered marginal for farming then it could be set aside to protect wildlife, regardless of whether or not the boundaries were in the right place; rather as the colonial powers carved out empires without any regard for the tribal affinities of the local inhabitants. Even though the governments that created them might have been paying no more than lip service to the ideal they espoused, the game parks and reserves were meant to be forever, a place where the animals would always be safe, where development was put on hold and indigenous people were resettled in deference to wildlife. Excluded from their former hunting grounds, however, traditional hunters felt alienated from the land and viewed the park's authorities as their enemies. To try to limit poaching, the

raising money for conservation. But it wasn't long before environmentalists began to voice concerns that mass tourism, with its legions of zebra-striped mini-buses, was damaging the environment. Eco-tourism became the buzzword, with the emphasis on fewer people paying more money and staying at environmentally friendly camps and lodges. This has worked well in places such as Botswana, where tented camps are small and no more than three vehicles can congregate at a predator sighting, and a similar approach is now meeting with considerable success on private conservancies in Kenya.

Meanwhile a wave of humanity was pressing closer and closer to the boundaries of the parks and reserves. Talk of the aesthetic value of wildlife and 'living museums' seems out of place when you are so poor that you often do not have enough to eat or struggle to find sufficient firewood to cook with. Poaching in all its guises intensified. Anti-poaching forces were no match for the highly organized and heavily armed motorized gangs, which decimated Africa's elephant and black rhino populations in the 1970s and '80s. In the last 40 years 95 per cent of Africa's 60,000 black rhinos have been killed, and during the 1980s the elephant population was cut in half – a loss of 600,000 animals. The ban on the ivory trade in 1989 certainly helped to buy time for the elephants. But the bush-meat trade has now reached staggering proportions throughout Africa. Game meat – antelope, buffalo, zebra – is readily available in many local butcheries. Populations of chimpanzees and gorillas continue to dwindle as the commercial logging companies open up Central Africa's last great tracks of rainforests, encouraging the meat hunters to move in.

Realizing that they were rapidly losing ground, conservationists in the 1980s and '90s began to focus their efforts on empowering local communities in an attempt to create a more positive attitude towards wildlife and provide economic

incentives to stem the tide. The Kenya Wildlife Service agreed to allocate some of its revenue to benefit people living in areas bordering the parks and reserves. These communities are the ones with the most to lose from wildlife: they must try to co-exist with potentially life-threatening animals such as the elephants and buffaloes that raid their crops, and the lions and leopards that kill their livestock. But some people feel that the priority for the Parks Service should still be to focus all their efforts and resources on protecting wildlife within parks and reserves, and with so little wild land remaining the interests of people must be secondary – an attitude doomed to failure. If the local people feel alienated from wildlife they cannot be expected to support efforts to preserve it. If only

The best places to see wild dogs are the Okavango Delta in Botswana, the Kruger in South Africa and the Selous and Ruaha in southern Tanzania.

powers that be ran the parks like military operations, adopting a fortress mentality. But the colonial governments were reluctant to provide much in the way of finances, and rangers and wardens did an admirable job under the most difficult circumstances.

The 1960s saw the dawning of greater environmental awareness. Parks authorities began to take a more balanced view of the role of predators (though the last wild dog shot by a ranger in the Serengeti was in the early 1970s). Hunting safaris for wealthy overseas clients were already in decline, replaced by photographic safaris as a way of

The enormous Selous Reserve (43,000km² or 16,600sq. miles) is an important sanctuary for lions and wild dogs, and probably has the largest single population of lions in Africa.

wealthy tourists can afford to visit parks and reserves, and only overseas hunters can legally shoot wildlife for pleasure – not even for food – it is bound to seem inequitable to people who see little benefit from these forms of land use and who live in abject poverty.

In countries such as South Africa and Namibia game-ranching and trophy-hunting have long been seen as a way for landowners to earn money from wildlife while helping to conserve it. This is only possible if the state enacts laws that give people control over wildlife on private land, either by ceding ownership to them or by granting them the right to use wildlife, which is not yet the case in Kenya. It may be unpalatable to some, but a 'use it or lose it' philosophy is now considered by many people as the only way for wildlife to survive.

How do lions fit in with this new scenario? Wherever large tracts of land have been fenced off to ranch cattle and/or game, such as in Namibia and South Africa, lions have been eradicated. And whenever lions move out of protected areas onto communal grazing land herdsmen are quick to take action to prevent them from attacking livestock – regardless of the fact that some predators never do. Even large protected areas set aside specifically to safeguard wild animals are increasingly under pressure, as we have seen in the Masai Mara. Lions and other large carnivores also find themselves compromised by illegal meat-hunters, who set wire snares that kill indiscriminately. When lions, hyenas and leopards try to scavenge from animals caught in snares, the meat-hunters respond by lacing carcasses with poison. And predators get caught up in the snares themselves (they have proved a real threat to Zimbabwe's endangered wild dogs). Some manage to escape by chewing through the wire, but in the process may pull the wire so tight around their neck that it cuts through their windpipe.

In the Serengeti–Mara ecosystem, where the bushmeat trade is big business, Angie and I have seen lions or hyenas with injuries such as these or a hyena running around on three legs having chewed its foot off to escape from a snare. And in areas where trophy-hunting concessions border parks and reserves, lions are sometimes lured across the park boundary with strategically placed bait by hunters eager to bag a fine-maned male, a complaint that was voiced to us over and over again as we travelled around Africa in search of big cats. Controlling incursions into protected areas in whatever form – pastoralists, meat-hunters or trophy-hunters – is always going to be difficult. Patrolling vast tracts of land effectively is prohibitively expensive and most African governments simply don't have the financial resources to cope. Which is why it is so important to win the support of local communities – and the professional hunters.

For years, people have highlighted the plight of Africa's endangered cheetah population, which is currently thought to number anything from 12,000–15,000 animals. They have rightly focused attention on the devastating impact the trade in fur skins had on the world's spotted cats in the 1960s and '70s – in some countries it is still a major concern. Though the leopard survives in good numbers in parts of Africa and in Asia, it is threatened in many areas where it used to be abundant. But it is only very recently that people have begun to wake up to the fact that there are far fewer lions today than there were 20 years ago, and realize how fragmented the population has become. Lions need large areas to find sufficient food. A single pride of lions generally requires a home range of 50–100km$^2$ (20–40sq. miles) and a healthy lion population is considered to be one with around 100 breeding pairs, or 500 or more lions in total. The Masai Mara sustains such a population, but there are very few places remaining like the Mara. At the present rate

of decline, lions will soon become extinct over large parts of Africa; in places they already have.

The African Lion Working Group (ALWG) has been trying to assess how many wild lions are left on the continent. They started their survey by targeting Central West Africa, where virtually no long-term studies of lions have been undertaken. The response to questionnaires was so good that ALWG expanded the exercise to the whole subcontinent. Not very long ago it was estimated that there might be between 50,000 and 100,000 free-ranging lions roaming the African plains. Now it seems likely that 30,000 – possibly fewer – is closer to the truth, with numbers in West and Central Africa even lower than feared with perhaps as few as 2,000 lions. Currently it is estimated that only five areas remain with lion populations of 1,500 adults or more – Serengeti–Mara (3,000), the enormous 43,000km$^2$ (17,000sq. mile) Selous Game Reserve in Tanzania (perhaps 3,750), Kafue complex in Zambia, Northern Botswana (2,500) and the Kruger National Park and adjoining private game sanctuaries in South Africa. Other parks and reserves famous for their big cats, such as Ngorongoro Crater in Tanzania, Samburu National Game Reserve in Kenya, the South Luangwa National Park in Zambia and Etosha National Park in Namibia number lions in their hundreds.

Recovery for small isolated populations of large predators is possible if sizeable portions of wild habitat with good prey densities are protected, so the population can eventually expand. The Asiatic lion has recovered from fewer than 100 individuals to around 300, and the Amur or Siberian tiger population dipped as low as 30–40 individuals in the 1940s, but clawed its way back to an estimated 350 adults and 100 subadults and cubs by the mid 1990s. But simply saving habitat isn't enough. Without adequate prey populations the predators cannot survive, as they are forced to leave the safety of parks and reserves to seek alternative prey. If food is scarce then taking livestock is their only alternative. And that means conflict with man in a battle that the predator cannot win.

One of the lion's remaining strongholds is Botswana, which over the last 30 years has become the focus of attention for many of the issues involving the long-term survival of wild lions – loss of suitable habitat, conflict with livestock owners and the impact of trophy-hunting. Mark and Delia Owens highlighted many of these issues in *Cry of the Kalahari*. An area of concern they shared with other conservationists was the number of lions and other predators being killed by humans. With lion numbers diminishing in many parts of Africa, hunting them for sport might seem more of an anachronism than ever, unless the trophy-hunter was able to shoot a problem animal that had been taking livestock.

There is no doubt that trophy-hunting can have a negative impact on lion populations unless it is strictly monitored, just as it did 25 years ago in the Masai Mara. When Kenya banned hunting in 1977, poaching was out of control and trophy-hunting had fallen into disrepute. Until then appeals by the World Wildlife Fund (now the World Wide Fund for Nature) for reduced hunting quotas had fallen on deaf ears. The majority of Kenya's hunters adhered to the principles set out by the Professional Hunters Association to try to ensure that the killing of trophy animals was done as humanely as possible; that wounded animals were always followed up; and that quotas where strictly adhered to. But some hunters blatantly ignored these principles with the connivance of corrupt game officials. By the time the ban was announced it was difficult to find a mature male lion in parts of the Masai Mara. The East African Wildlife Society visited the Mara in 1976 to survey a 8km (5 mile) radius around Governor's Camp – the same area where *Big Cat Diary* is filmed and where the Marsh Lions of that time were forced to live without pride males. Their findings confirmed what everyone knew – that lions and leopards were being shot illegally in and around the reserve, and that the lion population was seriously compromised by a complete dearth of big, mature males.

Certainly the ban on hunting helped to reverse the fortunes of the Mara's lions. And it didn't end there. For a number of years people had been voicing their concern about the government's policy of 'maximum consumptive utilization' of wild animals through hunting and game-ranching. Three months after banning hunting, Kenya prohibited the sale of all wildlife products, giving Nairobi's 200 curio shops three months to dispose of their stocks of animal skins, ivory carvings, horns and elephant-hair bracelets. One reason why Kenya has never reopened trophy-hunting or game-ranching (except on a very limited basis) has been the fear that it

Scruffy play-fighting with one of the young Marsh Lions. Adult lions play more often when they are getting plenty of food.

One of the Topi Plains Pride males being greeted by a six-month-old cub. The breeding life of a male is short, and some only ever get one chance of holding a pride.

would simply open the door to over-utilization and abuse of the system, providing a convenient loophole for the trade in wildlife products from endangered species. Kenya sees tourism as the most appropriate way to benefit from its wildlife resource, and the issue of whether to allow consumptive use of wildlife is still unresolved.

For most people the thought of shooting a lion or a leopard simply to display it as a trophy or for the enjoyment of hunting it seems indefensible. Lions spend much of the daytime sleeping, and sometimes they

don't even get to their feet unless prompted to, particularly if they are used to vehicles and have come from a protected area. But trophy-hunting is an expensive business, costing tens of thousands of dollars, and most clients want to be sure of getting their lion. So instead of days of tracking and missed opportunities, bait is put out to attract the lion to where the hunter can easily shoot it. If the rules are obeyed the client is driven no closer than 200m (220yd), steps down from the vehicle and fires before the alarmed animals can make their escape.

A lion rarely charges when it sees a human on foot. Its first impulse is to flee, as I have witnessed so many times in the Mara whenever the Marsh Lions catch sight of Masai walking in their direction (or hear them), acknowledging an ancient fear of human beings. But if a lioness has cubs or a male is courting a female, then they may well charge, though nine times out of ten this is bluff and as long as the person doesn't run, but carefully backs away, they will almost certainly escape to tell the tale. An injured lion is an entirely different proposition, and at that point the professional hunter must follow it up and dispatch it. Most hunting accidents occur with wounded animals.

Sadly there is another way of hunting a lion. 'Canned' hunting, as killing captive lions has become known, is a lucrative industry in South Africa. Canned means 'in the can' – literally a dead certainty as far as the lion is concerned, and there are places – farms or game-ranches – offering such trophy lions for the taking. Not a wild lion that might just have the chance to escape, but a lion incarcerated in a fenced-off enclosure. In one well-publicized incident the lion was drugged beforehand, so that

by the time the client arrived it simply sat there rather than moving off and unduly taxing the hunter's ability to hit the mark. Though some might argue that at least this saves the life of a wild lion, surely both man and animals deserve to be treated with dignity. As George Schaller said, 'Every hunter who feels the need to prove himself by obliterating a lion, who strives to have his name in the obituary column of a trophy book, should contemplate his intended victim for a while. There hopefully will come a time when, possessed by a feeling of fellowship, he can no longer kill for pleasure.'

Adult males make up a relatively small part of the lion population (around 20 per cent), so hunting quotas should always be on the conservative side. Unfortunately it is very difficult for a hunter to know if he is shooting a pride male or a nomad – and finding a male on his own does not necessarily mean he is not part of a coalition controlling a territory. The rationale that trophy-hunting weeds out the old, non-breeding animals from a population – as is often argued with buffaloes, for instance – cannot be applied to lions. A trophy lion with a big mane is likely to be a prime breeding male, and part

Elephants drinking at the Luangwa River, Zambia. Due to poaching for ivory, Africa's elephant population halved during the 1980s, with a loss of 600,000 individuals.

of a pride. As we saw when Scruffy was killed, the repercussions from the loss of such a male can be severe – in that instance they reverberated through the Marsh Pride for well over a year.

The Serengeti Lion Project currently has a student studying the impact of trophy-hunting in the Maswa Game Reserve, adjacent to the Serengeti, to discover if prides in hunting blocks suffer an increase in takeovers due to loss of pride males. If hunting is killing males on a more frequent basis, cub survival could be so low that the pride eventually dies out. One suggestion put forward to try to counteract the disruption that hunting has on the life of a pride, is that when a male is killed there should be no further lions shot in that area for a minimum of two years. This would allow time for new males to integrate with the pride and for their cubs to survive long enough to escape infanticide.

Robin Hurt, a well-known professional hunter based in Kenya, has operated for many years in the Maswa area and has made a concerted effort to prevent illegal hunters from working his concessions and to empower the local people. Over the last ten years Hurt and an American hunter and conservationist, Joseph Cullman, have brought benefits worth more than £250,000 to 18 village communities adjoining some of Tanzania's game reserves and game-management areas, on the condition that the communities concerned help to prevent poaching. Hunting clients pay 20 per cent over the government licence fees to support the scheme. Under these circumstances, hunting can be seen both to benefit local communities and to help maintain wildlife areas, regardless of how distasteful it might seem. But any benefits have to be balanced against the impact on the game populations. Only when the Maswa lion study is completed will we have a better idea of what that is, allowing hunting quotas to be set on a more scientific basis.

Wildebeest in the Moremi Game Reserve, Okavango Delta, Botswana. The delta is often described as the jewel of the Kalahari and rivals the Serengeti–Mara as a wildlife spectacle.

In Zambia, where trophy-hunting is currently banned, one old-timer commented to us recently, 'Hunting quotas are arbitrary; lions and leopards are lured from the parks with baits; rangers are not paid on time, so it is tempting – and much more lucrative – to be a poacher rather than a gamekeeper; and most villagers living close to the parks and game management areas think of them primarily as sources of meat.'

Meanwhile some years ago neighbouring Zimbabwe initiated one of the most highly publicized success stories in community conservation. Campfire (Communal Areas Management Programme for Indigenous Resources), as it became known, aimed to encourage the local population to view wildlife in a more positive way, primarily through the revenue accruing to them from trophy-hunting and game-ranching. Apart from the bonus of providing a meat harvest when a hunting client shot an elephant, Campfire prompted the local people to play a far more pro-active part in preventing

poaching in their areas by instilling a sense of ownership and of protecting their own assets. Sadly recent political events in Zimbabwe have put back the cause of conservation by years. Repossession of ranches has led to widespread killing of wildlife for meat and trophies – rhino horn and ivory – and inevitably compromised the work of privately owned conservancies. As always, poverty and greed are the great killers of wildlife.

In 2001 the anti-hunting lobby won an important victory. Having originally made a quota of 53 lions available to the hunting industry, the Botswana government announced a moratorium on lion hunting. One of the main reasons for the ban is said to have been concern voiced by wildlife researchers over the number of lions being trapped and shot by cattle owners in northern Botswana. In 2000 more than 80 lions were reported to have been killed in this area, along with hyenas, leopards and cheetahs. Further south, in the Kgalagadi District, 93 lions were killed between 1997 and 2001. Initially the ban was intended to prevent farmers from shooting 'problem' predators, but in order not to appear to be favouring the trophy-hunting industry it was decided to extend it to cover all lions.

Concerns over the impact that feline immuno-deficiency virus (FIV) might have on lion populations may also have played a part in the decision. FIV causes AIDS in domestic cats, first producing flu-like symptoms from which the cat seems to recover before succumbing three to five years later to a breakdown in its immune system; this leads to a lethal combination of gut infections, skin lesions, respiratory infections and wasting. FIV has been found in 25 species of the cat family, all thought to carry their own strain. It is prevalent in certain populations of wild lions, such as those in the Serengeti and Mara, where 80 per cent carry the virus with no signs of ill health, implying that it has been around for a long time. Old viruses are good viruses in as much as they haven't killed off their host, with whom in time they evolve a symbiotic relationship. Researchers speculate that FIV may have been present for million of years, perhaps first infecting the ancestor of all modern cats and then spreading to other species, which would account for the fact that they seem to carry different strains.

Transmission of the virus in lions is probably not through sexual contact, birth or suckling. Rather, the high infection rate among lions compared to their more solitary relatives is probably a reflection of the number of times lions get cuts and bites in social squabbles or at kills. Cheetahs rarely use physical violence at kills (though groups of males sometimes attack singletons) and leopards don't share food at all. The passage of FIV from one species of cat to the next has probably come about by an infected cat being attacked by another – or even eaten. Leopards occasionally kill and eat cheetahs, and lions attack both species as competitors, though they rarely eat them.

But not all lions have FIV. Only 12 per cent of the Kalahari lions studied by Paul Funston tested positive, perhaps because the population is so dispersed, and of the 44 lions sampled in Namibia none carried antibodies to the virus; neither did Asian lions or tigers. The fact that the FIV strain found in domestic cats tends to be lethal means that it is almost certainly a recent disease in this species, perhaps within the last 1,000 years. Similarly, the human immuno-deficiency virus (HIV) that often leads to AIDS is thought to be no more than 200 years old, which is why it is so deadly. It may even have mutated over millions of years from FIV via the simian form of the virus, SIV, found in primates. Thousands of years later, perhaps through the bush-meat trade, the virus passed to humans and mutated into HIV.

Lions are susceptible to a number of viral diseases, such as feline herpesvirus and feline parvovirus, neither of which has a marked impact on the population. But viruses certainly can have lethal consequences for cats, as the outbreak of canine distemper – a disease that primarily affects members of the dog family – proved in the Serengeti–Mara between 1993 and 1995. Over 85 per cent of the Serengeti lions were infected, and a third of the population – 1,000 lions – as well as jackals, bat-eared foxes and wild dogs died within a year. The source of the disease was domestic dogs living in villages around the western boundary of the park, part of the 100,000 dog population encircling the Serengeti–Mara ecosystem. They would have passed it to hyenas, who act as carriers as they commute from one area to another, mingling with other predators at kills. Canine distemper is a brutal disease, with stricken animals sometimes lingering for

**It is not uncommon to see lions resting in trees in the Mara, particularly during the wet season when the grass is long – this provides a convenient perch from which to look for prey or locate their companions.**

days, even months, and often suffering repeated brain seizures before eventually dying. That the majority of the lions survived is due to the fact that in the early 1980s they had experienced an outbreak of the disease that had gone unobserved until blood samples detected its presence. A programme to vaccinate the domestic dog population against rabies and distemper was initiated in 1996 and is continuing.

Dr Pieter Kat and his partner Kate Nicholls have been studying lions in the Okavango Delta region of Botswana, which is thought to have between 1,200 and 1,600 lions. They have repeatedly voiced

concerns about the impact of trophy-hunting on the lion population and the role that FIV might play if the lions are unduly stressed. Because the virus is constantly mutating there is no reason to think that it never harms lions or that some day one of these new strains might not prove lethal. Kat and Nicholls welcomed the hunting ban, and feel that until more research has been done on Botswana's lion population it should be given full protection.

But while the killing of lions by trophy-hunters for 'sport' steals the headlines, it pales by consideration to the impact of anti-predator sentiment among farmers and ranchers. In places such as Botswana, increased efforts are now being made to mediate with local communities affected by predator-livestock issues. Attempts to educate people on the benefits of protecting predators are balanced by more short-term solutions such as removing, relocating and as a last resort killing problem animals.

One of the biggest complaints voiced all over Africa is the lack of compensation by the government for stock losses. But compensation schemes are beset with difficulties. An upsurge in claims since compensation was offered in Botswana has been countered by accusations that not all of the claims are valid. The ranchers and local communities respond by saying that the amount of compensation has failed to keep up with current prices for livestock, and that often the wildlife authorities are slow to respond to calls for help, forcing landowners to take action and kill the predators themselves. A lion can wreak havoc among domestic stock and may kill a number of animals. Unless decisive action is taken quickly the cost can be prohibitive to the smaller farmers.

But not all lions are stock-raiders, as has become apparent from the Laikipia

Predator Project in northern Kenya. Lions identified as stock-raiders were radio-collared and tracked by vehicle and plane, rather than being shot. It turns out that certain lions never become stock-killers and that some forms of herding practices and boma systems are more effective at deterring lions than others. More substantial stockades and houses could be constructed to ensure that lions did not break in. If they did, then paying compensation would be justified. A sturdy boma of thick thornbushes is preferable to the chicken-wire enclosures favoured by some of the more modern herders. These are easy for the lions to see through and simple for a determined predator to penetrate. Bomas with minimal human presence are far more vulnerable to lion attack. When herders build their dwellings close to their cattle bomas the noise and general activity make it far less tempting for a lion to approach unless it is really desperate. Livestock could and should be herded back into an enclosure at night, and the calving period should be synchronized rather than taking place throughout the year (and frequently out in the bush).

Simply shooting every lion that trespasses on private land, regardless of whether or not it is a stock-raider, may fail to solve the problem. Instead it may open up an opportunity for other predators to fill the vacuum, without necessarily dealing with the culprits. Most large predators will scavenge from a carcass killed by another predator or one that has died of disease or drought, and may be unfairly blamed for the death. This is one reason why baiting and trapping of predators should be strictly controlled, thereby avoiding the indiscriminate killing and maiming of animals that haven't damaged livestock. Tolerating predators may in some circumstances be to the rancher's advantage, helping to maintain a natural balance between predator and prey.

Non-territory holders – often young lions – are in many cases the ones that become habitual killers. Lions who leave parks and reserves during the dry season to try to find food should, where possible, be captured and returned to the reserve rather than killed, and greater effort should be made to patrol and maintain fences. But once a really determined and persistent stock-raider has been identified it must be removed (perhaps as new breeding stock for one of the private game sanctuaries) or destroyed, preferably by government officials, not the rancher – and only on proof that the predator has actually killed their livestock. In countries where the sale of skins is permitted, the money could be put into a fund to compensate ranchers.

None of this might seem to have much relevance as we prepare to film another series of *Big Cat Diary*, certainly not for people watching the big cats living out their lives on television screens far away from Africa. Angie and I can feel the excitement rising as we start counting down the days, making sure our four-wheel-drive vehicles are going to be able to withstand the daily attrition of driving over rough roads and across country for ten weeks. Time to check our camera gear and hope that the long rains that have been pounding Kenya for the last few weeks haven't created a fungal bloom inside our telephoto lenses. There's talk of another el Niño in mid-October when the short rains begin, in which case we're going to need boats as well as vehicles to follow the big cats as the series draws to a close. By then we will be busy writing the next book in this series, *Big Cat Diary: Leopard*, with *Cheetah* to follow. The Mara will certainly be very different from when we last filmed two years ago, and Kenya was in the grip of a devastating drought. Fortunately, the Mara has so much to offer besides the big cats.

Meanwhile, our fridge is bursting with hundreds of rolls of film to carry with us to the Mara in August. Our heads are buzzing with questions. Will the Topi Plains males still be with the Marsh Pride, we wonder, and will some of the young Marsh females have rejoined the pride to stand side by side with Khali, Bump Nose and the other adult lioness to defend their ancestral territory? Discovering whether Solo has survived will definitely be part of our new adventure and will force us to dig out our notebooks and thumb through our photographs so that we can be sure of his whisker-spot markings. He was eight months old when we last saw him, a gangly youth sprouting the first signs of a mane and sporting a 'thick lip' from some altercation with his older pride mates. If he is still alive he will be just over two years old, and it will soon be time for him to leave his natal pride – perhaps he already has. But with no other males of a similar age to join him he is going to find life tough on his own, unless he can forge an alliance with another nomad, as Scruffy and Scar did. It will be even more of a miracle if Gimpy and her cubs have managed to cling to their old haunts since the loss of Red, their lives bearing stark witness to why it is so important for lions to form groups – and why we should be concerned for the future of these great cats.

My over-riding impression, having spent half a lifetime watching wild lions, is the degree to which the individual stands out. To me, characters such as Scruffy, Khali and the Marsh Sisters are so much more than mere 'animals'. As the top predator, lions represent wilderness perhaps more than any other creature I know. If we can find room for lions to roam free, it will ensure the survival of many other species. The idea that they might one day slip away is unthinkable.

**Being part of a pride in a stable, well-defined territory is essential if a lioness is to rear her cubs successfully. Only by protecting the wilderness they live in can we hope to ensure that the king of beasts continues to reign.**

# Gazetteer of big cat safari destinations

Setting out on a safari to Africa is the high point of many people's lives. For some it will be a journey of just a few weeks; for others it may mean the beginning of a new life, as it was for me when I left London in 1974 and joined a group of other young people travelling overland through Africa.

Most people who come on safari have high expectations, built on visions of wildlife captured in books or on television programmes such as *Big Cat Diary*. But these images can be deceptive, often relying on months or even years of waiting for the right moment, capturing events that happen only rarely. Consequently, when people arrive in the Mara they often expect – rather than hope – to see a leopard lounging in a tree in Leopard Gorge, to experience the thrill of having a cheetah jump on the bonnet of their car, or to watch lions pulling down a buffalo. But there are no guarantees about what you see on safari – just the promise that the experience will change you forever.

The biggest lesson Angie and I learned on our recent safari through southern Africa was to throw away our expectations and enjoy whatever came our way. We had chosen destinations that we hoped would give us the best chance of seeing big cats. Some were famous for leopards or cheetahs, others places where all the big cats were said to be on view. Not all of them lived up to their reputation, not because it was undeserved, but because what we had hoped to see had happened yesterday or last week.

Due to time considerations we visited Namibia,

Botswana, Zimbabwe, Zambia and South Africa in one continuous safari in the space of six weeks. The changing seasons can have a huge influence on what you see or don't see, so make sure you are travelling at the right time of the year for each destination when you plan your itinerary. If a place is 'good' for big cats, that implies that there's plenty for them to eat – the antelopes, gazelles, zebras and buffaloes on which they depend. By comparison with these prey species, predators are in the minority, so in looking for them you are guaranteed to find plenty of other animals to feast your eyes on. A safari is so much more than finding big cats. Nevertheless we have chosen places where we have experienced the best big cat watching. But our list is by no means exhaustive. There are many other areas out there waiting to be explored. Though lions are the focus of this book we have included all three big cats in this review. The Insight guide *African Safari* and the Lonely Planet guides to *Watching Wildlife in East Africa* and *Southern Africa* are a mine of information for safari travellers.

## Recommended destinations
### Masai Mara National Reserve, Kenya
(1,510km²/583sq. miles)

This is one of the best places to see all three big cats, particularly lions. The rainy seasons are mid-October through to December (short rains) and April to June (long rains). The grass is at its longest after the long rains, making it more difficult to find predators, though you are virtually guaranteed to see lions at any time of year. The migration of wildebeest and zebras usually arrives in June or July, with most of the

herds returning to the Serengeti by the end of October.

September through to the end of March is our favourite time in the Mara, as the long grass retreats under a wave of animals. The best time to witness the great herds crossing the Mara River is from August to October – so September is a good bet, but no two years are the same. Even when the wildebeest and zebras depart the Mara it is still a beautiful place to visit, and with the grass short (and green during the rains of October–November) it is easier to find predators. The drier the year the better the predator viewing; the grass and bush are eaten back and stripped bare, making it easier to get around and see what is on offer.

The Mara is a birder's paradise, with more than 500 species. For accommodation, try Governor's Camp, Mara Intrepids or Mara River Camp. The Mara Triangle to the west of the river is excellent for cheetahs, though they are found throughout the reserve, and Little Governor's Camp, Olonana and Serena Lodge are among the best places to stay in the Triangle. If you prefer a private tented camp, East African Wildlife Safaris and Abercrombie and Kent are among a number of safari outfitters offering this option in Kenya.

### Samburu National Reserve, Kenya
(104km²/40sq. miles)

One of the smaller reserves, but what a gem, providing a taste of northern Kenya, with excellent bird life. Any safari to Kenya should include a visit to Samburu. The scenery makes a wonderful contrast to the lush, rolling plains of the Mara, with stark rocky outcrops, dry bush country with towering termite mounds, and the palm-fringed Ewaso Nyiro River. To the south of the river lies Buffalo Springs National Reserve, which is equally good.

The dry seasons are best in Samburu, with plenty of activity around the river and large herds of elephants emerging from the forests to drink and cross. There are Grevy's zebras, gerenuks and reticulated giraffes – dry-country species that you don't find in the Mara.

Samburu and Buffalo Springs are famous for their leopards, and some of the camps and lodges put out bait in the evenings to attract nocturnal visitors. But you are quite likely to see leopards here during the day. There are lions and cheetahs, too, and wild dogs are occasionally seen. Among the best places to stay are Larsens tented camp, Mara Intrepids and Samburu Serena Lodge.

### Serengeti National Park, Tanzania
(14,763km²/5,700sq. miles)

The Serengeti would be worth a visit even if it didn't have any wildlife. The fact that it does – in the kind of abundance found in few other places – makes this one of our top five wildlife destinations worldwide.

The sheer expanse of the Serengeti plains, particularly in the rainy season when the massed herds of wildebeest and zebras darken the grasslands, is a sight to behold, with lions, hyenas and cheetahs all in attendance. The wildebeest cows give birth to their calves between January and March, so February is a good time to visit. The wildebeest leave the plains and head for the woodlands and water at the beginning of the dry season towards the end of May, streaming in their thousands through the spectacular Moru Kopjes. The more marked the transition between wet and dry seasons, the more dramatic the exodus from the plains. This is when the wildebeest begin their rut, and it is well worth heading for the Seronera area in the centre of the park, which has always been one of Africa's top leopard haunts. They frequently lie up among tall stands of yellow-barked acacia trees along the Seronera Valley or slump contentedly along the broad beam of a sausage tree. Seronera is also a good place to look for lions and cheetahs.

The rugged northern woodlands around Lobo are another good place to visit when the great herds are passing through in the dry season (June–October). Among the best places to stay when the herds are massed on the southern plains are Ndutu Lodge, overlooking Lake Lagarja, and Kusini Camp; with Serengeti Sopa Lodge within easy reach of Moru, Serengeti Serena Lodge a good base in the centre of the park, and Klein's Camp for the Lobo area.

## Ngorongoro Crater, Tanzania

(260km²/100 sq. miles)

The eighth wonder of the world, and certainly worth stopping for two nights, not only for its unique geological features and stunning views, but also as home to some striking black-maned lions. You will be lucky to see cheetahs here, though you might catch sight of a leopard among the forests. The crater is an excellent place to view the endangered black rhino, with the ink-blue backdrop of the crater wall making the perfect scene-setter for wildlife photography. The birdlife is excellent, and the magnificent bull elephants with their long ivory tusks are always a favourite. If you are a keen photographer, or just want to get the best out of your stay, be sure to take a picnic breakfast as well as lunch. The misty morning atmosphere and chances of finding lions on the move make it well worth being out early.

Of the three lodges, Sopa Lodge provides the easiest access to the crater floor, while Ngorongoro Serena Lodge offers all 75 rooms with crater views. If you just want luxury and fine food, it might almost be worth spending the day in your room, with a view to match, at the Ngorongoro Crater Lodge.

## Selous Game Reserve, Tanzania

(43,000km²/16,600sq. miles)

Tanzania's southern wilderness is the place to take a walking safari in East Africa. This is 'old' Africa, wild bush country that harbours more than 100,000 buffaloes, nearly 60,000 elephants, the highest density of wild dogs anywhere in Africa and probably the largest single population of lions – with fewer tourists watching them. Even though the lions are not as numerous or as easy to see as in places such as the Mara and Serengeti, a visit to one of the tented camps along the Rufiji River is an ideal starting point for a walking safari. A boat trip along the river to watch giant crocodiles, large pods of hippos and elephants is a must, or you could simply take time out back at camp, to catch up with identifying some of the more than 440 species of birds.

Among the best of the camps are Sand Rivers Selous (particularly for those wanting to walk) and Selous Safari Camp (formerly known as Mbuyuni tented camp). A safari combining a visit to Selous and Ruaha National Park, and either Mahale Mountains or Gombe National Park to see chimpanzees, would be a great adventure away from the hustle and bustle of Tanzania's northern tourist circuit. But if it is easy wildlife watching that you want and your first fix of Africa, then Serengeti, Ngorongoro and Tarangire (1,360km²/525sq. miles), with its magnificent baobabs, large herds of elephants, excellent birdlife and a good chance of seeing lions and leopards, are hard to beat.

## South Luangwa National Park, Zambia

(9,050km²/3,500sq miles)

Known locally as the Valley, this is where Norman Carr, one of Africa's most experienced safari guides, pioneered walking safaris. The Luangwa River dominates the park, providing a cooling and tranquil element. With the camps and lodges situated along the riverbanks, you can spend hours at a time watching the various animals coming to drink from the veranda of your tent – elephants, buffaloes, pukus, waterbucks, even lions and leopards. The best game-viewing is during winter (May–August) and the dry, hot months from September to November. Game concentrations tend to increase as the dry season progresses, but so too does the temperature. The rains (November–April) are excellent for birding, though most of the lodges and camps close at this time. The density of leopards is exceptional and lions are frequently seen. We visited in September, and during a night game drive – a highlight of any visit to Luangwa – saw one of the leopards that helped to make this area famous. Apart from looking for big cats, we spent many hours photographing elephants drinking and crossing the river, and enjoyed close-up views of the spectacular colonies of carmine bee-eaters that nest in the sandy banks.

There are a number of outfitters offering walking safaris, but Robin Pope Safaris is consistently recommended. The ideal time is probably late June to late September, for a five-day walk with a top guide, staying at mobile tented camps deep in the bush. Robin and Joe Pope also run three of the best permanent camps in the Valley: Nsefu, Tena Tena and Nkwali. A walking safari – even if only for a morning – is a must.

## Kafue National Park, Zambia

(22,480km²/8,680sq. miles)

The second largest national park in Africa, comprising vast tracts of woodland and savanna bisected by the Kafue River. Surprisingly few people visit Kafue, considering that it is home to large herds of elephants, buffaloes, lions and leopards, and is renowned for its diversity of antelopes, with floodplains brimming with thousands of red lechwes and glimpses of magnificent sables and roans. There are cheetahs and wild dogs here, too, with large prides of lions hunting buffaloes on the Busanga Plain in the north. The animals tend to concentrate around water between July and October, with Busanga best between August and October.

There are only a handful of lodges, adding to the sense of wilderness. Among the best are Ntemwa and Busanga Bush camps, situated in the middle of the plains where lions are often seen; Lufupa Camp is well located for game drives and bush walks, with the chance of seeing leopard on night game drives.

## Mana Pools National Park, Zimbabwe

(2,200km²/850sq. miles]

It is hard to think of Zimbabwe without planning a visit to the spectacular Victoria Falls and overnighting at the grand Victoria Falls Hotel. This is the place to take a canoe safari down the mighty Zambezi River, which forms the northern boundary of Mana Pools National Park. Hippos, crocodiles, elephants and buffaloes are all easily seen here. Mana is a likely spot to see lions, as is Matusadona National Park, which stretches up from the shores of Lake Kariba, and both offer the chance to walk or canoe, an exciting alternative to being driven around the African bush. John Stevens was one of the pioneers of canoe safaris and is one of Africa's top guides, specializing in walking and canoeing safaris, during which guests stay in mobile tented camps. Musangu and Muchichiri are two pleasant riverside lodges offering permanent accommodation, with Wilderness Safaris' Rukomechi and Chikwenya camps also highly recommended.

If you visit Lake Kariba, then Sanyati Lodge is among the best – you can relax, enjoy the lake and strike out on game drives, walks or fishing trips.

## Moremi Game Reserve, Botswana

(3,900km²/1,505sq. miles)

The Okavango Delta is a huge oasis, an inland delta of wooded islands and papyrus swamps, whose crystal-clear waters disappear among the Kalahari sands. The delta rivals the Serengeti and Masai Mara as a wildlife spectacle, with excellent lion- and leopard-viewing, and a good chance of seeing cheetahs and wild dogs. The combination of water and wildlife is hard to beat, and the big-game viewing and birding opportunities are virtually limitless. The Moremi Reserve encompasses almost one third of the delta, and includes Chief's Island. The autumn/winter dry season (April–September) is best for wildlife viewing. There is an excellent chance of seeing wild dogs in June and July when they abandon their nomadic wandering for a few months and establish a den. Game-viewing reaches a peak during September and October, when animals congregate around permanent water, though temperatures can be high.

Many lodges close during the rainy season (December–March). There is a huge selection of camps and lodges to choose from, but among the best are Chief's Camp in the Mombo area, and Wilderness Safari's camps, Mombo and Little Mombo.

A visit to the Okavango Delta also offers the possibility of walking safaris, horseback safaris, even elephant-back safaris at Randall Moore's Abu's Camp, and a chance to walk with Doug Groves's elephants at Stanley's Camp. In the north, and bordering Namibia, Chobe National Park (11,700km²/4,520sq. miles) is home to large prides of lions and huge herds of buffaloes, and offers river trips to watch elephants crossing the Chobe River. In the west of the park, the Linyanti Marsh and Savuti areas are famous for their lion-viewing, though it can be very seasonal. Chobe is a good place to visit en route to Victoria Falls, stopping over at Chobe Chilwero Lodge.

## Okonjima and the Africat Foundation, Namibia

(135km²/52sq. miles)

Namibia is home to more cheetahs than any other African country, with perhaps 3,000 of these elegant cats. But 90 per cent are found on private ranchland, where they often run into conflict with ranchers. Lise Hanssen and her team at the Africat Foundation have dedicated themselves to working with ranchers to lessen conflict with predators, removing animals that are trapped and might otherwise be shot or poisoned. They work mainly with cheetahs and leopards, but also with servals, caracals and the occasional lion, supporting a number of research and education projects. The Hanssens have turned the family home at Okonjima ranch into comfortable guest accommodation, providing visitors with the chance to visit the Africat Foundation and meet some of the cheetahs. Photographers will find plenty of interest here, and a

visit to the leopard blind in the evening is an experience not to be missed.

## The Cheetah Conservation Fund (CCF), Otjiwarongo, Namibia

CCF was the brainchild of Laurie Marker and Daniel Kraus, and is dedicated to the long-term survival of the cheetah through research and education. Laurie and her team are at the hub of cheetah conservation and, like the Africat Foundation, work closely with ranchers, providing a home for orphaned cheetahs trapped on ranchland. CCF has pioneered the use of guard dogs to help farmers reduce stock losses to predators, and has placed well over 120 Anatolian Shepherd dogs with farmers. Where possible wild-caught adult cheetahs are relocated. The excellent Visitor Education Centre at CCF is open to the public.

To see wild cheetahs in Namibia, the best option is to visit Etosha National Park (22,270km²/8,600sq. miles). Natural springs and artificial waterholes (such as the Okaukuejo waterhole) dotted along the southern edge of the stark Etosha Pan at the heart of the park provide the focal point for game-viewing, attracting large numbers of animals, such as wildebeest, zebras, springboks, gemsboks and elands. Though all three big cats are found here, there is no guarantee that you will see them. If big cats are the priority and time is short then perhaps this is not the place for you; otherwise it is memorable.

## Namib-Naukluft Park, Namibia

(49,754km²/19,210sq. miles)

This enormous wilderness stretches from Luderitz in the south to Swakopmund in the north. Not the place to see big cats, but as a safari destination it is a world apart, a vast moonscape with towering dunes, which are transformed when the summer rains come – if they come – in December to February. The extraordinary creeping welwitschia plants are endemic to the Namib and can live for more than 2,000 years. Sossusvlei Mountain Lodge in the adjoining Namib Rand Nature Reserve, and Wilderness Sossusvlei Camp are among the best, offering a variety of activities including day trips to the towering dunes of Sossusvlei. There is even a star-gazing safari with the help of a giant telescope at Mountain Lodge – not to be missed.

## Kruger National Park, South Africa

(19,480km²/7,520sq. miles)

This is South Africa's premier national park, with more mammal and bird species than any other park in the country. All of the 'big five' can be found here – lions, leopards, buffaloes, rhinos and elephants – as well as cheetahs and wild dogs, with the southern area of the park offering the greatest variety of landscape and the best game-viewing. The one big limitation has always been that you are confined to tarmac

roads. However, the parks authorities have recently put out to tender a number of private concessions, where off-road driving and walking safaris from small camps and lodges will add a whole new dimension to a safari in Kruger. Game-viewing is best during winter (May–October), when animals concentrate at water sources. The rainy season is from October to March.

## Sabi Sands Game Reserve, South Africa (including Londolozi and Mala Mala)

(650km²/250sq. miles)

There are a number of private game reserves clustered along the western boundary of the Kruger that are no longer separated from it by fencing. These offer excellent opportunities for big cat enthusiasts, and are particularly worth a visit if your passion is leopards. The most famous is Londolozi (130km²/50sq. miles), which has been transformed by John and Dave Varty since they took over the lodge in the early 1970s and restored the area to its former glory. Also well worth a visit is Mala Mala – both of these virtually guarantee leopard sightings. When we visited Londolozi we saw three different leopards on five separate occasions, as well as three magnificent male lions and plenty of cubs, white rhinos, elephants and two glorious kudu bulls.

Night game drives are a feature at all the lodges, and a good way to see leopards, though the rangers work hard to track them down during daytime as well, with off-the-road driving the norm. Cheetahs and wild dogs are not uncommonly seen. Ngala, Sabi Sabi, Singita and Idube lodges are all recommended.

## Phinda Resource Reserve, South Africa

(180km²/70sq. miles)

Lions and cheetahs have been introduced to this private game reserve, and it is certainly a good place to photograph them – particularly cheetahs, which are almost guaranteed. But getting a clear view of them usually depends on being able to drive off-road, and this is restricted after annual burning, so be sure to check first. All the 'big five' are here, and leopards are quite often seen. Winter (May–October) is the dry season and the best time for clear sightings. Accommodation at Phinda is in four luxury lodges. Phinda offers a number of extensions. You can opt to walk in search of black rhino in the adjacent Mkuzi Game Reserve, dive on the east coast coral reefs or fly over Greater St Lucia Wetland Park.

# Further Information: Bibliography

## Websites

**African National Parks**
HYPERLINK http://www.newafrica.com/national-parks/

**Africat** (Lise Hanssen's project)
HYPERLINK http://www.africat.org/

**Cheetah Conservation Fund**
(Laurie Marker's project)
HYPERLINK http://www.cheetah.org

**Big Cats Online**
dialspace.dial.pipex.com/agarman/bco/ver4.htm

**Big Cat Research**
www.bigcats.com/

**IUCN Cat Specialist Group**
lynx.uio.no/catfolk

**The Lion Research Centre** (lions of the Serengeti and Ngorongoro Crater)
HYPERLINK http://www.lionresearch.org

**Friends of Conservation**
(conservation body involved in the Mara)
HYPERLINK http://www.foc-uk.com

## Tour Operators

**Abercrombie and Kent**
(East and southern Africa)
HYPERLINK http://www.abercrombiekent.co.uk

**Afro Ventures** (East and southern Africa)
HYPERLINK http://www.afroventures.com

**Conservation Corporation Africa**
(East and southern Africa)
HYPERLINK http://www.ccafrica.com

**East African Wildlife Safaris** (Kenya)
HYPERLINK mailto:eaws@kenyaweb.com

**Gibb's Farm Safaris** (Tanzania)
HYPERLINK mailto:ndutugibbs@nabari.co.tz

**John Stevens Safaris**
(Zimbabwe canoe/walking safaris)
HYPERLINK mailto:bushlife@hare.iafrica.com

**Okavango Tours and Safaris**
(Botswana)
HYPERLINK http://www.okavango.com

**Richard Bonham Safaris**
(Tanzania – Selous specialist)
HYPERLINK
mailto:Bonham.Luke@swiftkenya.com

**Robin Pope Safaris**
(Zambia – Luangwa Valley specialist)
HYPERLINK mailto:popesaf@zamnet.zm

**Wilderness Safaris**
(southern Africa specialists)
HYPERLINK mailto:outposts@usa.net

**Governor's Camp**
(Kenya/Masai Mara tented camps)
HYPERLINK mailto:info@governorscamp.com

**Worldwide Journeys and Expeditions**
(African safari specialists)
www.worldwidejourneys.co.uk

It would have been impossible to write this book without leaning heavily on the work of other authors. We're particularly grateful to Judith Rudnai, here in Nairobi, for generously sharing with us her experiences of studying lions – and her library of books and articles. To Jim Cavanaugh for his time – and his dedication to the future of the Nairobi Park lions. To Gus Mills at Kruger Park in South Africa for his fund of knowledge on Africa's large predators and for providing copies of scientific articles. To Pieter Kat and Kate Nicholls for stimulating company at their camp in Botswana, where they study lions. To Luke Hunter, who worked on the lion and cheetah reintroduction project at Phinda in South Africa and who was incredibly generous with his time, as well as providing invaluable information and many contacts among predator researchers working in southern Africa. To Laurie Marker and her team at the Cheetah Conservation Fund in Namibia for their patience and hospitality when we visited their project. To Lise Hanssen and the Africat Foundation – and the Hanssen family at Okonjima in Namibia – who were equally helpful and welcoming. And to Johan Naude and Sarel van der Merwe of the African Lion Working Group (IUCN/SSC) for their tireless work in promoting the cause of lion conservation and for providing me with copies of Vols 1, 2,and 3 of *African Lion News* (the official newsletter of ALWG), published between May 2000 and Aug 2001.

From its first inception, the Serengeti Lion Project has provided a steady stream of scientific information on wild lions, enabling us to source numerous scientific papers and popular accounts. Though published 30 years ago, *The Serengeti Lion* by George Schaller still stands as a landmark among books on field biology, combining science and eloquence in equal measure. More recently, *Into Africa*, Craig Packer's first-hand account of a life working with lions and baboons, rattles along like a detective novel, providing humour and insight into the joys and hardships of fieldwork in East Africa. The results of Craig's work, and that of his co-workers and students, figure prominently in this text.

We are only too well aware of the dangers of misinterpreting the work of others, particularly when trying to present information gleaned from scientific papers. Accordingly, while we are indebted to the following authors, they remain blameless for any inaccuracies in our text, and we apologize for the inevitable simplifications in interpreting their work.

Adamson, J. *Born free: the full story*, Pan Books: London 2000

Ames, E. *A glimpse of Eden*, Collins: London 1968

Angier, N. 'Please say it isn't so, Simba: the noble lion can be a coward' *The New York Times*, 5 September 1995

Bertram, B.C.R. *Pride of lions*, J.M.Dent: London 1978

——*Lions*, Colin Baxter Photography Ltd: Grantown-on-Spey 1998

Bull, B. *Safari*, Viking Penguin Inc: New York 1988

Cooper, S.M. 'Optimal hunting group size: the need for lions to defend their kills against loss to spotted hyaenas', *African Journal of Ecology*, Vol. 29: 130-136, 1991

Cowie, M. *Fly Vulture*, George G. Harrap & Co. Ltd: London 1961

Creel, S. & Creel, N.M. 'Lion density and population structure in the Selous Game Reserve: evaluation of hunting quotas and offtake', *African Journal of Ecology*, 35: 83-93, 1997

Estes, R.D. *The behavior guide to African mammals: including hoofed mammals, carnivores, primates*, The University of California Press: Oxford, England 1991

Fitter, R., & Scott, P. *The penitent butchers*, Collins/FPS: London 1978

Funston, P.J. 'On the edge: dying and living in the Kalahari', *Africa Geographic*, September 2001

Funston, P.J. & Mills, M.G.L. 'Aspects of sociality in the Kruger Park lions: the role of males', in *The Proceedings of a Symposium on Lions and Leopards as Game Ranch Animals*, Onderstepoort, October 1997

Funston, P.J., Mills, M.G.L., Biggs, H.C., & Richardson, P.R.K. 'Hunting by male lions: ecological influences and socioecological implications', *Animal Behaviour*, 56, 1333-1345, Article No. ar980884 1998

Grzimek, B, & Grzimek, M. *Serengeti shall not die*, Hamish Hamilton: London 1960

Guggisberg, C.A.W. *Simba: the life of the lion*, Howard Timmins: Cape Town 1961

Hanby, J.P., & Bygott, J.D. *Lions share: the story of a Serengeti pride*, Collins: London 1983

Harvey, C and Kat, P. Prides: *Lions of Moremi*, Southern Book Publishers: New Holland 2000

Herne, B. *White hunters: the golden age of African safaris*, Henry Holt & Company, Inc: New York 1999

Hunter, L. 'Pride of Phinda', *BBC Wildlife*, Vol. 16, No. 10, October 1998

—— 'Tooth and claw: the future of Africa's magnificent cats', *Africa Geographic*, Vol. 9 (5): 46–56, 2001

IUCN Cat Specialist Group. 'Hope for lions', *New Scientist*, Vol. 172, issue 2317, 17 November 2001

Iwago, M. *In the lion's den*, Chronicle Books: San Francisco 1996

Jackman, B.J. *Roaring at the dawn: journeys in wild Africa*, Swan Hill Press: 1995

——'Cat watching, Africa: lions, leopards and cheetahs: where to see them', *BBC Wildlife*, Vol. 19, No. 2, February 2001

Jackman, B.J., & Scott, J.P. *The Marsh Lions*, Elm Tree Books: London 1982

——*The big cat diary*, BBC Books: London 1996

Kat, P. 'The lore of lions', *BBC Wildlife*, Vol. 18, No. 1, January 2000

Kingdon, J. *East African mammals: an atlas of evolution in Africa*, Vol. 3, part A (Carnivores), Academic Press: London 1977

Klum, M. 'Asia's last lions', *National Geographic*, Vol. 199, No. 6, National Geographic Society: June 2001

Latter, Y. 'Laikipia predator project: radio-collared lions', *Travel News*: Nairobi, May 2001

Leopold, A. *A Sand Country almanac: and sketches here and there*, Oxford University Press: Oxford 1987

Liebenberg, L. *The art of tracking: the origin of science*, David Philip Publishers: Claremont, South Africa 1990

Lopez, B.H. *Of wolves and men*, Charles Scribner's Sons: New York 1978

Macdonald, D. *The velvet claw: a natural history of the carnivores*, BBC Books: London 1992

Marchant, J. 'Lions in peril', *New Scientist*, Vol. 172, issue 2315, 3 November 2001

Mellon, J. *African hunter*, Cassell: London 1975

Michler, I. 'Botswana's great lion debate', *Africa Geographic*, Vol. 9, No 9, October 2001

Mills, G., & Harvey, M. *African predators*, Struik Publishers: South Africa 2001

Morell, V. 'The killer cat virus that doesn't kill cats', *Discover*, July 1995

Moss, C. *Portraits in the wild: animal behaviour in East Africa*, Elm Tree Books: London 1989

Neff, N.A. *The big cats: the paintings of Guy Coheleach*, Harry N. Abrams, Inc: New York 1982

Nowell, K., & Jackson, P. *Wild cats: status survey and conservation action plan*, IUCN/SSC Cat Specialist Group, IUCN: Gland, Switzerland

Ogutu, J.O. 'Test of a call-in technique for estimating lion (*Panthera leo*, Linnaeus 1758) population size in the Masai Mara National Reserve, Kenya', Moi University, M.Phil.thesis: Nairobi 1994

Ogutu, J.O. & Dublin, H.T. 'The response of lions and spotted hyenas to sound playbacks as a technique for estimating population size', *African Journal of Ecology*, 36:83-95 1998

Owens, M, & Owens, D. *Cry of the Kalahari*, William Collins: London 1985

Packer, C. *Into Africa*, University of Chicago Press: Chicago & London 1994

Packer, C., & Pusey, A.E. 'Divided we fall: cooperation among lions', *Scientific American* magazine, May 1997

Packer, C., Scheel, D., & Pusey, A.E. 'Why lions form groups: food is not enough,' *The American Naturalist*, Vol. 136, No. 1, July 1990

Patterson, G. *To walk with lions*, Rider: London 2001

Pennycuick, C.J., & Rudnai, J. 'A method of identifying individual lions *Panthera leo* with an analysis of the reliability of identification', *J. Zool. Lond.* 160: 497-508

Pickford, P., & Pickford, B. *The miracle rivers: the Okavango & Chobe of Botswana*, Southern Book Publishers: South Africa 1999

Pringle, J. *The conservationists and the killers*, T.V Bulpin and Books of Africa (Pty) Ltd: Cape Town 1982

Rudnai, J. 'Reproductive biology of lions (*Panthera leo massaica* (Neumann)) in Nairobi National Park', *East African Wildlife Journal*, 11:243-251

——*The social life of the lion: a study of the behaviour of wild lions (Panthera leo massaica (Neumann)) in the Nairobi National Park, Kenya*, Medical & Technical Publishing Co Ltd: Lancaster, England 1973

——'The pattern of lion predation in Nairobi Park', *East African Wildlife Journal*, 12:213-22

Schaller, G.B. *The Serengeti lion: a study of predator-prey relations*, University of Chicago Press: Chicago 1972

——*Serengeti: a kingdom of predators*, Collins: London 1973

Scheel, D., & Packer, C. 'Group hunting behaviour of lions: a search for cooperation', *Animal Behaviour*, 41, 697-709 1991

Scott, J.P. *The leopard's tale*, Elm Tree Books: London 1985

——*The great migration*, Elm Tree Books: London 1988

——*Painted wolves: wild dogs of the Serengeti–Mara*, Hamish Hamilton Ltd: London 1991

——*Kingdom of lions*, Kyle Cathie Ltd: London 1992

——*Dawn to dusk: a safari through Africa's wild places*, BBC Books in association with Kyle Cathie Ltd: London 1996

——*Jonathan Scott's safari guide to East African animals* (revised & updated by Angela Scott), Kensta: Nairobi 1997

——*Jonathan Scott's safari guide to East African birds* (revised & updated by Angela Scott), Kensta: Nairobi 1997

Scott, J.P., & Scott, A. *Mara–Serengeti: a photographer's paradise*, Fountain Press: Newpro UK Ltd., London 2000

Seidensticker, J., & Lumpkin, S., (eds). *Great cats: majestic creatures of the wild*, Merehurst Ltd by arrangement with Weldon Owen Inc: London 1991

Shales, Melissa. *African safari*, Discovery Communications Inc: 2000

Smuts, G.L. *Lion*, Macmillan South Africa: Johannesburg 1982

Turner, A., & Anton, M. *The big cats and their fossil relatives: an illustrated guide to their evolution and natural history*, Columbia University Press: New York 1997

Turner, M.; Jackman, B.J., (ed). *My Serengeti years*, Elm Tree Books: London 1987

Whitfield, P. *The hunters*, Hamlyn: London 1978

Willock, C. *Wildfight: a history of conservation*, Jonathan Cape: London 1991

Winterbach, C.W., Winterbach, H, Sechele, M.L., Kat, P.W. *Coordinated dry season lion survey for the Okavango Delta* 1999, published June 2001

# Acknowledgements

We have received such generous support from so many individuals and companies that it is possible to mention only a few of them here.

We would like to thank the governments of Kenya and Tanzania for allowing us to live and work in the Serengeti–Mara, and to acknowledge the assistance of Tanzania National Parks, and the Narok and Trans Mara County Councils, who administer the Masai Mara National Game Reserve. Over the years Senior Wardens John Naiguran, Simon Makallah, Michael Koikai, Stephen Minis and James Sindiyo in the Mara and David Babu and Bernard Maregesi in the Serengeti have all been helpful and supportive of our projects.

Thanks to everyone involved in *Big Cat Diary* (BCD), both here in Kenya and at the Natural History Unit (NHU) in Bristol. To 'field commander' Keith Scholey and series producer Fiona Pitcher, for supporting the idea of this book, and to Keith and his wife Liz, and Robin and Elin Hellier, for welcoming us into their homes whenever we visit the NHU. The success of BCD relies on people working together, and as much as anyone, Mandy Knight, production manager of BCD, epitomizes the combination of professionalism and big-heartedness that makes working on the programme such a privilege and pleasure.

Rosamund Kidmund-Cox, editor of *BBC Wildlife* magazine, has been a good friend and great supporter of our work over the years, and helped us believe that there was room for yet another book on lions.

Myles Archibald at HarperCollins commissioned this series of three titles featuring Africa's big cats, beginning with *Lions* (we are now hard at work on *Leopards*). His enthusiasm for the project helped to spur us on when time was of the essence. Katie Piper at HarperCollins added a calming influence, for which we are most grateful. And a big thank you to Liz Brown for her design skills in crafting the book in record time.

Caroline Taggart has edited all but one of our books. By the time Angie and I arrived in London with tens of thousands of seemingly chaotic words on lions tucked under our arms, even someone as unflappable as Caroline realized that she was going to have to call on all her considerable editing skills – and an uncanny ability to make her authors feel that anything is possible – if we were to complete on time. How does she do it?

Mike Shaw, our literary agent at Curtis Brown, as always provided a safe pair of hands, and his assistant Jonathan Pegg was wonderfully supportive and managed our affairs with great charm and professionalism.

Our wildlife photographs are held by three picture libraries: NHPA, ImageState and Getty Images. Tim Harris and his team at NHPA generously allowed us to rifle the 'lion' files at short notice for this book, as did our great friend Jennifer Jeffrey at ImageState.

Both Angie and I have family living overseas who have been an unfailing source of help and encouragement. Now that my sister Caroline and her husband Andy have moved from England to sunny Portugal, my brother Clive and his wife Judith have kindly inherited the boxes of books and slides that used to live at Caroline's house in Inkpen. Angie's mother Joy still lives in England but sadly hasn't enjoyed the best of health recently, and her brother David and wife Mishi now live in France. We miss them all.

Pam Savage and Michael Skinner have taken us under their wing these past few years, offering advice and reassurance when needed, and allowing us the freedom of their home in London. It is difficult to know how to thank friends like that adequately. Cissy and David Walker have been equally forthcoming with their generosity and good fellowship. And Frank and Dolcie Howitt continue to be the best of neighbours to us here in Nairobi, and are very dear friends.

Many other people have provided us with a second home during our visits to England over the years, particularly Pippa and Ian Stewart-Hunter in London, Brian and Annabelle Jackman in Dorset, Dr Michael and Sue Budden in Buckinghamshire, Ken and Lois Kuhle and Martin and Avril Freeth in London, and Charles and Lindsay Dewhurst in West Sussex – all wonderful hosts and friends who put up with our comings and goings with admirable tolerance.

We have shared memorable times with our good friends Neil and Joyce Silverman in Africa, Antarctica and at their beautiful home in Florida. They have helped us in so many ways over the years, and are always there when we need them.

Carole Wyman has been a loyal and generous friend to Angie since they met in Kenya many years ago, and is godmother to our son David. Carole is an individual of rare qualities, and this book is dedicated to her.

Jock Anderson of East African Wildlife Safaris continues to be a great friend to our family. He gave me the chance to live at Mara River Camp 25 years ago, a gift of such magnitude that I shall never forget his role in making it possible. Stephen Masika, Jock's office messenger, still keeps track of correspondence and renews licences for us with unfailing efficiency.

Aris and Justin Grammaticus have been generous in allowing us to base ourselves at Governor's Camp, and Pat and Patrick Beresford and their staff at Governor's Workshop somehow manage to keep us on the road, regardless of the damage we inflict on our Toyota Landcruiser.

Finally, we would like to acknowledge the invaluable help of Shigeru Ito of Toyota East Africa; Allan Walmsley, formerly of Lonrho Motors East Africa; Canon Camera Division (UK); John Buckley and Anna Nzomo at Air Kenya; Mehmood and Shaun Quraishy at Spectrum Colour Lab (Nairobi); Pankaj Patel of Fuji Kenya; Redmond Walsh of Abercrombie and Kent (South African office); and Jan Mohamed of Serena Hotels, all of whom have made life in the bush tenable through their ongoing support.

We are truly fortunate in being able to follow our passion as a career. But the joy that this brings pales alongside the inspiration and love we derive from our children Alia and David. May their lives be equally blessed.

# Index